CW00347318

Marketing

Marsaili Cameron, MA, carries out writing and editorial work through her own business, Cameron & Hanscombe. Specializing in the preparation of distance teaching materials, she has worked for a wide variety of organizations, including the Open University. She has played a central role in the creation of customized training materials in marketing for several major British companies.

Angela Rushton, BA, Ph.D., M.Inst M., is director of Marketing Matters, a consultancy and training business. Prior to this she worked for a wide range of organizations, including Thorns, Texas Instruments, the Institute of Grocery Distribution and Cranfield School of Management. She has taught, written and broadcast widely on marketing matters.

David Carson, MBA, is Lecturer in Marketing Management at the University of Ulster. Prior to moving into education, he worked for several years in the textile industry. As an academic, he has concentrated his research and teaching activities on small businesses, working with small firms across a wide range of industries in Northern Ireland.

SERIES EDITORS: Stephen Coote and Bryan Loughrey

Marketing

Marsaili Cameron,
Angela Rushton
and David Carson

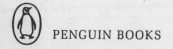

PENGUIN BOOKS

PENGUIN BOOKS

Published by the Penguin Group
27 Wrights Lane, London W8 5TZ, England
Viking Penguin Inc., 40 West 23rd Street, New York, New York 10010, USA
Penguin Books Australia Ltd, Ringwood, Victoria, Australia
Penguin Books Canada Ltd, 2801 John Street, Markham, Ontario, Canada L3R 1B4
Penguin Books (NZ) Ltd, 182–190 Wairau Road, Auckland 10, New Zealand

Penguin Books Ltd, Registered Offices: Harmondsworth, Middlesex, England

First published 1988
10 9 8 7 6 5 4 3

Typeset, printed and bound in Great Britain by
Hazell Watson & Viney Limited
Member of BPCC plc
Aylesbury, Bucks, England
Typeset in Linotron 202 Melior

Contents

List of figures

Acknowledgements

Many friends and colleagues gave us support and encouragement in writing this book. In particular, we would like to thank William Giles of Strategic Marketing Development Unit for many constructive comments and ideas – as well as for permission to use a number of diagrams; Sonja Ruehl and Tom O'Carroll for invaluable editorial help and suggestions; Margaret Reed for her patience with us and skill with the word-processor; and Lynn Carson and Dorrie Miles for their administrative assistance. As our editor, Stephen Coote has been a pillar of strength throughout the project; we offer him our most grateful thanks.

1 The Concept of Marketing

1 The Purpose of Marketing

What is marketing, anyway?

Exercise: What assumptions and beliefs do you hold about marketing? For example, is it about:

   (a) persuading as many people as possible to buy the product or service that your organization has already decided to supply?

   (b) making more memorable television commercials than your business competitors?

   (c) finding a way out of a short-term business crisis?

   (d) launching a new product or service?

   (e) making sure that your organization has someone called a 'marketing manager' or 'marketing director'?

   (f) making fast-moving consumer goods (like chocolate bars and household commodities) move even faster?

If you replied with a 'yes' to each of these questions, then the good news is that you're likely to find that marketing is in fact a great deal more interesting and varied in its scope than you assumed it to be. If you decided on a mixture of 'yes' and 'no' answers, then you can probably congratulate yourself on understanding that marketing is much more than just an 'add-on' to 'normal' business activity. If you answered the points with a list of 'no' responses, then you're likely to be aware that although some of the features mentioned above may be *included* in the marketing activity, none of them express the basic elements of the marketing concept.

So, what are these basic elements? They can be summarized as follows:

1. Customer orientation.   In the words of one marketing expert from Harvard Business School, Theodore Levitt, this means that every organization 'must learn to think of itself not as producing goods or services but as *buying customers*, as doing the things that will make people *want* to do business with it'.

2. Integrated marketing effort.   This recognizes the fact that marketing consists of many different functions which must be co-ordinated. These include:

> planning which products or services to market;
>
> the design, packaging and naming of the products or services;
>
> pricing;
>
> promotion through PR, advertising and sales promotion;
>
> distribution and physical presentation at the point of sale;
>
> after-sales service.

3. Prosperity-directed marketing.   Integration of effort and customer orientation are vital – but they are not enough. The ultimate aim must be an organization that achieves at least long-term survival and, preferably, long-term prosperity. This will mean different things to different types of organization. In the private sector, it means a profitable operation. Many firms sell increasing quantities of their products but make little profit – a kind of 'aimless prosperity'. A more selective marketing strategy can often improve this situation.

A useful short working definition of marketing can be found in Theodore Levitt's statement that marketing invariably views 'the entire business process as consisting of a tightly integrated effort to discover, create, arouse, and satisfy customer needs'.

Why bother with marketing?

What does all this mean in practice? Basically, it means that there is a continual matching process between a firm's output and customer requirements. This matching process occurs whenever there is a firm with paying customers. What varies is how conscious the firm is of the matching process and how well it manages it. In other words, while the process of marketing is universal, the degree of skill and planning with which this process is managed varies enormously from organization to organization.

Let us take a look at one example of an industry which suffered as a result of not taking the marketing concept fully on board – the Swiss watchmaking industry. For generations, Swiss watches enjoyed the reputation of being the best in the world – a reputation which bred complacency among Swiss watchmakers. When watches using the new microchip technology first appeared, this complacency led Swiss watchmakers to dismiss them almost out of hand as a serious source of competition. Most were also slow to accept the new technology. This initial failure to recognize the potential impact of the new technology on watch markets was, for some Swiss watchmakers, their last mistake. Others have survived, and have had to adopt the new technology to do so, but the delay has cost them their pre-eminence in many markets.

Handled differently, the technological developments that threatened the Swiss watch industry could instead have provided it with an opportunity. It could have been the first to adopt the new technology and to develop the markets for this type of watch.

This is something to remember. It is often all too tempting to try to ignore change or, if this is not possible, to see it in a negative light, as a threat, because change upsets the status quo. A more positive approach is to keep abreast of developments, so changes do not come as a surprise, and then accept, and even welcome, change for the opportunities it almost always brings with it.

Usually, marketing is about adapting to gradual yet continual change rather than coping with dramatic, cataclysmic change. An example of this may be found in the UK grocery industry. In the 1950s the Co-operatives brought self-service retailing methods to this country from the USA. It took some time for self-service to catch on, but it did – and with it came, first, the rise of the supermarket and, currently, the growth of superstores. Since the 1950s many grocers have gone out of business as a result of their failure to adapt to changing circumstances. Only those grocery retailers who have adapted their offering to best suit shopper requirements, and have stayed one step ahead of trends rather than one step behind, have survived and prospered.

All too often, however, businesses really appreciate their marketing problems and attempt to do something about them only when faced with a crisis. Let us examine the outlook for one firm of this kind – Jordan Electronics. This company makes electronic components and sub-assemblies for the electronics and electrical industries. A reputation for quality and reliability of service allowed the company to expand rapidly from a very small operation to a rather larger one – though still with a workforce of only twelve.

Before forming the business in 1983, the founder, William Jordan, had worked for a major supplier in telecommunications equipment. It was while he was employed there that Jordan had identified a market opportunity provided by the supplier's decision to sub-contract much of the sub-assembly work which previously had been carried out in-house. He took voluntary redundancy and established Jordan Electronics on the informal guarantee that he could satisfy his former employer's sub-assembly requirements. So, at the launch of Jordan Electronics, it was possible to describe it as a 'one customer' company, making sub-assemblies for telecommunications equipment.

At the end of the first year of operation, Jordan Electronics had gained only one other customer – rather than the three William Jordan had planned on. Around this time also, the supplier had begun to run into serious business problems, exacerbated by the loss of a major contract. Jordan's worst fears were soon realized when the supplier cancelled some sub-assembly contracts; as a result, Jordan was forced to lay off half his workforce.

Attempts to find replacement work failed miserably and William Jordan quickly came to realize that he knew little about what customers really wanted; accordingly, he felt at a loss when faced with having to identify and contact new potential customers. Previously, he had not given much thought to this side of his business; he had put off finding new customers because he had been so busy just running his business and because he had assumed that the task of finding customers would not be too difficult. Only at this point of crisis did he acknowledge his need to take the marketing concept on board.

Obviously a major potential weakness at the heart of Jordan Electronics lay in its over-reliance on one customer. This is a high-risk strategy which means that even an apparently thriving concern is vulnerable to running into severe difficulties in a short period of time.

Just as the 'one-customer' company is vulnerable, so too is the 'one product' company. You yourself will probably be able to call to mind a local small enterprise which came up with an excellent product idea, but which either failed to market it effectively or pinned too many hopes on its success. In recent years, many people have lost their redundancy money by putting it in less than carefully thought-out ventures involving the development of software items for the computer industry. And, in the medical field, one firm came up with an excellent prototype for improved dialysis equipment; but management failed to take into account the fact that in all developed countries, public expenditure on health had been cut back severely.

Exercise: Take a moment now to consider the factors that all these examples – both industry-wide and company-specific – have in common. You may find it helpful to group these factors under three different headings:

  (a) knowledge of customers;
  (b) awareness of market trends;
  (c) ability to meet customers' changing needs.

Initial appreciation of the value of marketing must be followed by a determined effort to grapple with the different factors involved. In an increasingly dynamic world, long-term survival depends on sound market information systems, the willingness of managers to anticipate change, and the ability of managers to make plans for an appropriate response.

More than one purpose

Let's go on now to look in greater detail at the different objectives which marketing can fulfil for an organization. These can be grouped under two headings.

Within the organization

Survival.   Marketing enables a company to survive by ensuring that the company's activities are acceptable and in demand in the market-place. Long-term survival depends on the organization's willingness and ability continually to identify, anticipate and meet the needs of customers.

Profit.   Where appropriate, marketing can contribute to profits by increasing volumes; generating revenue and cash; and adding value to products.

Development and expansion.   Marketing can enable an organization to anticipate and cope with change by adopting an outgoing and progressive approach. Through the constant upgrading of targets, marketing can lead the development and expansion of a company.

Outside the organization

Finding customers and markets.   Marketing aims to look for opportunities in the market-place; to 'feel the pulse' of the market; to stay – or to reach – one step ahead of the market.

Satisfy the market.   Marketing aims to provide the market with what it wants and needs.

Adapt and change, according to changing market needs.   Marketing ensures that, wherever possible, significant trends and events are anticipated and assessed. It also urges the organization towards adapting to new situations as they arise and planning for change so that opportunities can be capitalized upon and threats minimized.

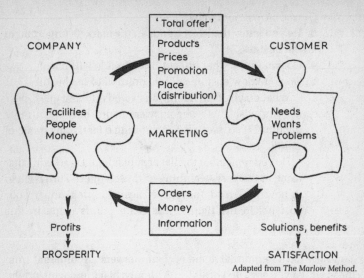

Figure 1.1.   The matching process

Develop wants.   Marketing can use its knowledge of trends in the market-place to develop new customer goals and desires.

Exploit opportunities.   Marketing can enable an organization to take advantage of market trends. It can organize, prepare and drive a company towards opportunities.

You will probably agree at this point that, looked at from whatever perspective, the purposes of marketing are fundamental to any organization. As Figure 1.1 shows, marketing matches the organiz-ational piece of the jigsaw with that of the customer.

Exercise: Now consider the following questions in relation to the business for which you work or a business which you know well.
1. Has the business made a major change to its products in the last three years? In your opinion, should change have been made? Why do you think this?
2. Has the business made a major change to its selling mes-sages in the last year? Do you believe that this decision

was a right one? Why?

3. Do you know the latest trends in the markets important to the business?
4. Do you know what impact these trends will have?
5. Do you know customers' real opinion of the business?

What do you feel, having answered all these questions? Do you wish that your answers could have been more detailed? If so, you are fast entering a marketing frame of mind!

Do you remember the list of beliefs about marketing that came at the very beginning of this chapter? Turn back to it now and read through it again, noting down your answers in the light of the main points made in this chapter.

You may have found that some of your answers are different from those which you gave first of all . . . Although black and white 'right' and 'wrong' answers are comparatively rare in the area of marketing, it may be helpful for you to compare your answers with the following comments from a marketing perspective.

(a) A marketing stance would always ensure that products and services are devised with the customers' needs clearly in view. This means that the decision to offer a particular product or service would be taken only if the prospective market could be shown to want it.

(b) Television advertising is only one possible element in an organization's marketing strategy. Marketing is concerned with *what* to market, *where* to market it, at *what price* to market it, as much as with *how* to promote and sell it.

(c) The development of a marketing approach *can* enable a business to survive a short-term crisis. However, if marketing is viewed in the first place as integral to the success of the business, then the organization is much less likely to need crisis management.

(d) Marketing is certainly needed in the design and launch of a new product or service. It would be a mistake, however, to assume that its role is confined to this. *All* products and services, as well as the organization's overall strategy, should be analysed in a marketing context.

(e) Unless the whole organization adopts a marketing approach, then the introduction or expansion of a marketing department is unlikely to bear the hoped-for fruit. An integrated effort is necessary to meet customer needs in the way most beneficial to the company.

(f) The marketing approach is just as relevant to industrial products (like heavy plant) and services (like banking and non-profit organizations) as it is to fast-moving consumer goods.

Checklist

For success in the market-place, all organizations need to check:

market trends

degree of market change

customer attitudes in general and those about the organization itself

what is currently happening in the market-place

what will happen in the market-place next year

their products' current suitability to the market-place

their products' future suitability to the market-place

the suitability of their selling messages in current and future market-places

whether they have sufficient new products on stream

whether they have sufficient new ideas for future products.

2 Using the Concept

Marketing – doing or thinking?

Exercise: Is marketing about *doing* things or is it about *thinking* things?

If you've responded to this question with a cautious 'both', then you're very much on the right track. Marketing is indeed both a set of activities – to be discussed in detail later in the book – and an approach to the business as a whole. Let us concentrate for the moment on looking more closely at what this approach involves.

There are several key elements.

Seeing the customer's point of view. First and foremost, a marketing approach to business means looking at everything an organization does from the point of view of the customer. A business, after all, can only stay in business in the long term by making sufficient sales – and this means keeping customers satisfied. It *should* follow from this that organizations ensure that any contact customers have with them builds and reinforces customer satisfaction. But does this in fact happen?

An organization may see no problem with, say, its accounting system. It may judge the system to be a good and efficient one, well geared to its needs. The organization's customers, however, may have many reservations about the way in which they are billed. They may find, for example, that the organization, which initially wooed them, presents a hostile and uncooperative face when queries are raised about invoices. So, after the marketing and sales personnel have expended much time, effort and money on making customers feel important, the accounting staff can make them feel little more than interfering nuisances for having the temerity to raise a query.

Of course, it is not only accounting staff who can be guilty of failing to look at themselves and their role from the customer's viewpoint. Staff involved in administration, production, distribution, after-sales service or any other area can, and often do, equally lack interest in what the customer wants.

Exercise: Can you think of a recent example where you, as a customer, felt that an organization had failed to live up to the promise offered by its marketing and sales side? How did you react to this incident? Will you remain a customer? How could the organization have avoided causing you disappointment or annoyance?

The moral is clear enough. Acceptance of the marketing concept means that everybody in the organization, regardless of job function or responsibility, must see their role as being primarily to service customers. If the organization is to achieve its goal of satisfying customer wants, then these customers themselves cannot be relegated to the position of second-class citizens who are, anyway, the responsibility of the marketing and sales function.

Good customer service can only be supplied if the customer's viewpoint is understood and appreciated, and if the organization actually encourages staff to put customers' requirements first. This will happen only if those at the top are genuinely 'customer-obsessed'. Instead of taking the blinkered view that their system works well for *them* as company employees, staff must be helped to consider how the system looks from the other side of the fence. Is it confusing for customers, for example? Does it present tedious complications for people – who are only concerned, after all, with purchasing a product or service?

One helpful way of judging this issue is to question the reasons behind the operation of any particular business system. Why does the system operate in the way it does? Is it in order to serve the needs of customers best? In many organizations the answer will frequently be: 'It works this way because . . . it always has/that's how the accountant likes it/our planning process needs it to work like this . . .' and so on, with no mention made of customers. Such answers show that the marketing approach has not yet filtered through these organizations.

A flexible, creative mind.   The 'marketing' frame of mind is characteristically flexible, outgoing, positive and creative. Many of us are by now familiar with Edward De Bono's concept of 'lateral thinking', which involves relating things or ideas which were previously unrelated. For example, asked to suggest some possible uses for a dictionary, a lateral thinker might offer many possibilities other than simply using it for checking the meaning of words. It could be used, for instance, as a step; or, with suitable modifications, as a hiding place for jewellery. This kind of creative thinking is central to an effective marketing approach. After all, most business environments are characterized by rapidly changing customer needs and desires and by intense competitive pressures. The organization which puts two and two together and makes five rather than a mundane four is therefore in a position of considerable potential superiority. Creative thinking is useful in nearly all areas of business activity, from product development to distribution strategy. Those banks which are currently pioneering the idea of home banking, for example – where financial transactions can be carried out on a home video screen – look set fair to capture much new and profitable business.

The creative thinker has little patience with the traditionally 'right' answers and solutions. He or she takes the time to play around with new angles and new approaches, no matter how irrelevant or impractical these may seem initially.

Have you had a creative idea during the last week? How did it come to you? What use could you imagine being made of it?

Open to new ideas and change.   Many people – whether or not they are in business – can recognize in themselves the propensity to resist advice or to reject new ideas. When they read, or listen to what others tell them, about how a problem can be solved, they tend to think, 'Ah, but it wouldn't work in my situation.' New ideas and suggestions for improvement in their business or work are met with negative and narrow responses.

What about you yourself? Can you honestly say you have never been in a position where you found yourself replying almost automatically, 'It won't work because . . .' If that situation *is* completely strange to you then you're in august company indeed – company which doesn't include the present authors!

A useful shorthand description of this negative approach to innovation is the 'Ah, but' syndrome. Often typified by negative words such as 'can't', 'won't', 'don't', 'mustn't', and so on, the syndrome can also be detected in other, softer, obstacle-creating comments such as, 'However, in our case . . .' In this mood, we can always find immediate reasons why new ideas – either our own or someone else's – will sink like a stone at birth.

Clearly, a negative approach of this kind is light years away from the frame of mind necessary for the effective marketing person. But, if we accept that this attitude exists, then what can we do about it? Just think what could happen if we consciously adopted a 'positive' attitude to business problems.

As an illustration, take the following example; it may be familiar to some of you.

Example: A friend suggests a new way of marketing your company. He recommends that you remodel your product range and embark on a different selling and advertising approach.

What is your instinctive reaction to this situation? It is likely to be one of two extremes. You may say, 'Ah, but it wouldn't work in my situation because . . .' or you may say, 'Thanks, I'll take a closer look at those ideas to see how they might be used.' Look at the gap between the two reactions. The first is negative; by adopting it, we instinctively close the door on any improvements and future progression; and, what is worse, we build a defensive rationale for doing so. The second, however, opens innumerable new avenues. Many of these we will later reject as not being feasible, but there is a possibility that one new avenue will lead to whole new horizons.

What then is the message for those interested in marketing? Always, regardless of the circumstances or the situation, be receptive to new ideas and suggestions. If only one in a hundred is feasible then it is one more than we had before we started.

If we build a wall of defence for what we have and refuse to listen to outside opinion, then we will seldom progress. We must make an effort to throw out negative words and phrases such as, 'but', 'I don't think so', 'it wouldn't work', and so on.

Don't look first for problems and pitfalls; look instead for possibilities and potentialities. Herein lies the difference between stagnation and decline on the one hand and progress and success on the other. Think positive, keep an open and receptive mind, and everyone will benefit.

Exercise: Take a moment now to list five 'positive' (progressive, forward-looking, constructive) actions or decisions taken by you this week. Now list five 'negative' (destructive, obstructive) actions or decisions taken during the same period.

How have the positive actions helped you in your work – and, in particular, in any marketing or selling responsibilities which you may have? And how have the negative actions helped you? What does a comparison between these last two answers suggest to you?

Commitment.   Creativity, enthusiasm and open-mindedness are all essential characteristics of the marketing approach. However, they are volatile qualities, liable to explode in a brilliant flash – and then disappear. If they are to make their full contribution to lasting marketing success, these qualities must be underpinned by other attributes, duller perhaps but just as valuable. Of these attributes, commitment and determination are the most important.

Running any business is beset by problems and setbacks of one kind or another. Managers are confronted daily with problems in trying to meet production schedules, in ensuring supplies or in maintaining reliable distribution and delivery. They also have to deal with constant customer inquiries and complaints. There may even be hiccups in sales that raise question marks over the marketing strategy adopted.

Under these circumstances it is not surprising that managers can and do waver in their faith in the course they have chosen and in their resolve to see it through. Many stop trying new things or generating new ideas because the last ones didn't seem to work.

However, what is ultimately needed is a manager both sufficiently flexible and receptive to accept essential change and determined enough and committed enough not to be easily deflected from the course he or she has adopted. Considerable measures of determination and resolve are in fact required to tackle problems and see new ideas through to a fruitful conclusion. Having decided on an objective which is based on a clear understanding of what is needed, the successful marketer must display a full commitment to doing everything necessary to achieve that objective.

Exercise: You may like to spend a minute or two here thinking about your own capacity for commitment. For example, have you ever started something (a course of study, for instance, or a DIY project) and never finished it? If, like most people, you have to answer 'yes', then you may care to go on to consider the reasons for your failure to carry the project through. Might they have included one or more of the following factors?

You didn't really think the project through in the first place.

You didn't anticipate the problems that arose or plan ways of overcoming them.

You didn't set achievable objectives along the way.

You didn't give yourself enough space to approach the task properly.

Just as factors like these can affect the attainment of personal goals, so they can damage commitment to marketing objectives. Careful thought and proper planning can make successful commitment, if not easy, then at least a much more likely proposition.

Checklist

The marketing approach to business demands that you:

make a conscious effort to approach marketing problems from the point of view of the customer

develop your capacity for creative thinking

consider ways in which you can avoid giving an immediate 'Ah, but' response to new ideas

look first for possibilities and potentials rather than problems and pitfalls

commit yourself to overcoming obstacles on the way to your chosen goal.

3 The Scope of Marketing Activity

Thinking marketing – then doing it

The marketing concept is an approach to business which stresses the importance of focusing on the customer. The *process* of marketing involves all the activities which are needed for a firm to organize itself so that its output matches the requirements of the markets it serves.

The marketing environment

This matching process, which is the essence of marketing activity, does not take place in a vacuum, sealed from all the factors and elements which make real life hazardous and unpredictable. Both the firm and its customers are continually influenced by a wide range of factors which, directly and indirectly, affect the relationship between them.

You may find it helpful to think of this wider context as the *marketing environment*. By and large, the elements of this environment are beyond the control of individual firms – or, indeed, of industries – but since they can exert a powerful influence on a firm's activities they require careful analysis and monitoring.

What kind of factors go to make up the marketing environment? Most organizations find it helpful to analyse their environment under the following general headings:

Economic conditions. The rate of inflation, taxation policy, interest and exchange rates, government regulation of the money supply and so on, affect both the level of customer demand and the ability of the firm to respond to that demand. In times of recession, for example, high levels of unemployment are likely to mean that 'luxury' products and services will appeal to a smaller market than would have existed in previous years.

Political and legal issues and developments.   Government policy can have a substantial impact on firms' marketing activities. Disincentives, for example, may be applied to trade with certain overseas countries; while incentives may be offered to particular types of firm in particular parts of the country. Firms operating within the European Economic Community (EEC) are subject to extensive legal constraints drawn up both by the EEC itself and by the individual nation states involved. Other countries, and groups of countries, also impose constraints appropriate to their circumstances.

Social conditions and trends.   The birth rate, changes in life expectancy, marriage patterns, migration both outside and within the country, are all relevant to most firms' marketing planning. An ageing population, for example, will present different marketing opportunities from those likely to be found in predominantly young or middle-aged markets. And any firm which fails to appreciate that in Britain today most women have expectations and responsibilities beyond the home is likely to run into trouble.

Technological developments.   Few markets today remain unaffected by rapid technological change; and those that currently do are unlikely to remain so for much longer.

In thinking about this area, it is worth remembering that the microchip, though immensely important, is not the foundation of *all* technological innovations.

The physical environment.   Terrain and climatic conditions are also important influences on demand and supply. Manufacturers of thermal wear, for example, benefit hugely from a prolonged cold spell; while UK hoteliers suffer badly from a series of cold summers.

Having analysed the relevance of broad trends like these to its own particular areas of interest, the firm will then want to focus on more specific factors.

Competition, The immediate questions about competition concern direct competitors – that is, other organizations providing the same or similar products and services. Who are they? How well are they doing? What marketing policies are they implementing? These are just a few examples of the questions to which answers should be sought.

However, in many markets, indirect competition can be even more threatening – especially in the longer term. Take the airlines, for example: where business travel is concerned, they face fierce indirect competition from the railway networks as well as from the new, improved methods of telecommunications that obviate the need for business travel at all.

Customers. Careful scrutiny must be given to the size and growth profile of markets; the buying behaviour displayed in these markets; and the underlying wants and needs of the customers. Every firm should aim to know their customers inside out.

Fashions. Many consumer markets are subject to the whims of fashion and hence exhibit violent upward and downward swings in demand. But fashion also affects other less obvious markets.

Exercise: Take a moment now to test your understanding of the marketing environment that surrounds your own business or a business well known to you. Answering the following questions will give you some idea of how well you understand it.

Do you know the current rate of inflation in the economy?

Do you understand the ways in which variations in the inflation rate affect your business?

Is the economy currently in boom or recession? What criteria do you use to decide this? How will the state of the economy affect your business?

Which major items of legislation affect your business? Are there likely to be changes in this area?

Can you think of three major social changes that have occurred in the last three years? Can you predict one major social change likely to occur in the next three years?

What major technological developments have occurred in your industry during the last three years? What new developments are likely to occur?

Who are the two major competitors in your industry? What are their main strengths and weaknesses? What kind of indirect competition do you also face? How do you know this?

What are the five main changes in your customers over the past three years? How have these changes affected your customers' buying behaviour in relation to your firm's products? What is likely to be the single most significant change in customers over the next two years?

The 'total offer' and the marketing mix

Having looked at the largely uncontrollable elements of the marketing environment, let us turn now to consider those marketing factors which *are* within the firm's control.

Essentially, the marketing concept of customer orientation and satisfaction means providing customers with a 'total offer' – a package of benefits which meet their wants and needs. This total offer will be more than just a product; customers rarely buy on the strength of a product alone. Products also need to be available at the right time and place; the price must be right; and customers need to know about them and believe that they will meet their needs, which means that customers have to be told about products in an informative and persuasive fashion. Put another way, the total offer has to comprise the right *product*, at the right *price*, in the right *place* and supported by the right *promotion*. These four elements of the total offer are often described as the *marketing mix* or, for obvious reasons, the 'four Ps'.

These four aspects of the marketing task can be broken down into many separate sets of activities.

Exercise: Take a look now at the following list of activities and decide with which 'P' each one is likely to be associated: research; development; planning and design; pricing; packaging; sales and sales management; advertising and sales promotion; public relations; distribution; after-sales service; trade discounts.

Most marketing professionals would arrange the list in the following way:

> **Product:** research, development, planning and design, packaging, after-sales service

> **Price:** pricing, trade discounts

> **Place:** distribution, service levels, after-sales service, packaging

> **Promotion:** sales and sales management, advertising and sales promotion, public relations, packaging

Note that 'packaging' and 'after-sales service' can occur in more than one place. For example, depending on the nature of the product being marketed, the packaging can prove to be an integral part of the product itself as well as a promotional tool. It may also provide essential protection for a product in transit and thus become a facet of distribution, the activity associated with the 'place' component of the mix.

It is often the case that a single activity can be categorized under more than one 'P'. The important thing to remember is that the four 'P's offer a framework which can be useful in helping and guiding marketing thought. The marketing mix is not intended to be a forum for academic discussion on the 'correct' placing of each element. A rough guideline for use is that if certain marketing activities seem to be related to more than one 'P', then they should be analysed under each of these headings. The only serious mistake lies in omitting to analyse an activity because it can't be fitted neatly into the existing scheme.

You may find it helpful to think of these four 'P's and their associated activities as marketing *tools* or *technologies*, to be used in the light of information gleaned from analysis of the marketing environment. To take a simple example – if a firm has discovered that most of its key customers prefer to come to their buying decisions through discussion with a salesman, then the firm will probably be well advised to concentrate its promotional effort on personal selling activities rather than on mass advertising.

Manipulation of any of the elements of the marketing mix is likely to affect customer demand for the product. Furthermore, since all these elements are interrelated and work together, a change in one will automatically have repercussions on, or implications for, all the others. It is absolutely essential therefore that there should be integrated and co-ordinated management of the whole marketing mix. Work on one 'P', however good, will be at best relatively ineffective and at worst counterproductive if it does not tie in with, and take account of, the situation in the other three 'P's.

Putting it all into practice

How in practice do companies successfully 'mix their ingredients' to achieve a satisfactory marketing result?

Let's look first at Company A, a manufacturer of machine tools. Analysis of their markets has shown them that their customer base consists of relatively few customer organizations, all of whom are deeply concerned that the products they buy should be highly reliable in use. After all, malfunction of the product would be likely to lead to a highly expensive shutting-down of the production line. Company A therefore decides on the following allocation of its marketing effort:

Product: Strict quality control which tests every machine tool prior to dispatch against a set of criteria developed from the main customer's definition of reliability.

Price: Key customers are relatively price-insensitive, and willing to pay for reliability. Hence, prices are at the top of the range, around 10–15 per cent above the middle-range 'average' price.

Place: Reliability in meeting delivery dates is more important than offering the shortest delivery time. Hence, the firm now works on guaranteed dates of delivery.

Promotion: Personal selling is the most important promotional tool, backed up by trade promotions and exhibitions. The reputation of the firm being also important to customers, the company must make every effort to stress its high standing.

Our second example is Company B, a manufacturer of convenience foods. This company is faced with the challenge of marketing its products both to its end users (the customers in shops) and to its trade customers – a variety of retail outlets. Failure to devise an appropriate marketing strategy for either of these groups of customers will result in the collapse of its marketing effort. If the shopkeepers are not convinced that the public will want to buy the foods, then they will be unwilling to stock them in the first place. If the customers do not both like the idea of the foods and see them attractively available in convenient shops, then they will not buy them. Company B therefore makes the following marketing decisions about Berrybar, a new fruit-based snack food.

Product: Berrybar is a product which works in with the trend towards natural, healthier snack foods. Close enough in concept to existing products to be acceptable, yet different enough to be new and exciting – to the trade as well as consumers.

Price: The snack market is very price-sensitive, partly because the retailers are very price-conscious. It is therefore decided to price Berrybar at the top end of the established price range for snacks. Standard trade margins are taken into account.

Place: The main outlets suitable for Berrybar are confectioners and grocers. These outlet types do not like keeping stocks so require frequent, reliable supplies.

Promotion: Media advertising is used to persuade end users that Berrybar is new, exciting and tasty – worthy of a try. Packaging needs to reinforce this message with point-of-sale promotion (such as retail displays) to remind and further encourage the customer to pick up the snack and buy. Efforts are also made to sell the idea to trade buyers. Major concerns are notified of the launch through personal visits.

Exercise: Our third company, Company C, is in the catering business and is anxious to find an appropriate marketing mix for one of its restaurants. The catchment area for this restaurant has gradually been changing in character, and the clientele has moved from predominantly family groups to groups of young, mainly single, professional people. Using the headings of the four 'P's, as in the examples above, jot down some notes on where you might expect Company C to direct its marketing effort.

Do your notes reflect our feeling that Company C should think seriously about changing the external appearance and interior decoration of the restaurant ('product'); the price at which menus are offered ('price'); the nature of the menus ('product'); and the image of the restaurant as reflected in all promotional materials ('promotion')?

The main message of this chapter can be summed up in a nautical image. Think of the marketing environment as the ocean and the firm's marketing effort as a ship on that ocean. The captain (the marketing manager) must continually consider the influence of currents, tides, waves and weather on his craft's progress to her destination, and he must be equally sensitive to the ways in which his vessel is likely to respond to any variations in these conditions. This means that he must know the strengths and weaknesses of his ship's design, shape, size and style intimately. The similarity between the two ventures ends here, of course; unlike the captain, the marketing manager is at liberty to change in mid-ocean the composition of his marketing mix. However, careful forward planning should make it less likely that he will be forced into abrupt, emergency changes of course.

Checklist

Before any marketing activities are set in train, you must:

analyse the marketing environment, paying particular attention to such factors as:
  economic conditions
  political and legal issues
  social conditions and trends
  technological developments
  competition
  customer variables

identify the 'total offer' which will be most attractive to your key target markets

analyse how this 'total offer' can be broken down into separate sets of marketing activities

find a way of integrating and managing the whole marketing mix so that the firm's output matches the requirements of the markets it serves.

4 Marketing in Context

The corporate environment

The marketing environment – made up of the external forces which impinge on the firm – is not the only backdrop for the marketing activity. The other setting in which the marketing function exists is the organization itself. This *corporate environment* is characterized by both formal and informal features, each type frequently having a profound influence on the way marketing develops within the firm.

Consider for a moment a question that is often put by bewildered onlookers: is 'sales' part of 'marketing' or is 'marketing' part of 'selling'? From a marketing perspective, the answer is simple: with selling forming part of the 'promotion' element of the marketing mix, all sales activity falls under the marketing banner. However, in practice, many firms had a sales function long before 'marketing' came on the scene and was formally introduced. As a result, their organizations are often set up in such a way that 'sales' operates as a separate function, with 'marketing' given the role of a promotional and support service for the sales teams. In many cases, this has proved fertile ground for intra-organizational feuding – a subject to be discussed later in the chapter – although, increasingly, the arguments for marketing to be treated as an integrating, overall activity have come to gain the upper hand.

At this point, it is important to remind ourselves that the *process* of marketing – that is, the matching of business output with customer requirements – is not a new phenomenon. Long before the term 'marketing' became common business parlance, firms were looking at market needs and trying to meet them. In the past, however, the process was carried out mainly on the basis of intuition and guesswork. The comparatively recent introduction of 'marketing' meant a formal recognition of two main things:

> the concept of customer orientation and satisfaction

> the range of activities involved in undertaking the 'match-ing' process that achieves customer satisfaction.

Where the organization is small and offers few product-lines, mar-keting can take its place fairly easily in the organizational context. After all, many owner-manager entrepreneurs are themselves in charge of all the main business functions and so are free to allocate time and resources as they think fit. However, in a large organization, a whole range of pressures and constraints, arising not out of the market-place but from the organization itself, can be brought to bear on marketing decision-making. The present chapter will concentrate on exploring the nature of this corporate environment.

Most large organizations separate their activities into four basic business functions: production, finance, personnel, and marketing. Sometimes this compartmentalization has the unfortunate effect that marketing is viewed simply as 'what the marketing function does'; the implication being that the rest of the organization is absolved from coming to grips with the marketing approach to busi-ness. However, the more positive aspect of compartmentalization is that there is a set of activities which comprise the process of market-ing, and it is very often the best organizational solution to place them together within a functional area.

Exercise: Think back now to what you've already learned about marketing and note down any features which seem to you to differentiate marketing from the other functions mentioned.

In your list you may have included the fact that the marketing func-tion has to be particularly sensitive to factors external to the organiz-ation, such as market trends; whereas the other functions may be influenced only indirectly by external factors. You may also have noted down that marketing must be concerned with *all* the activities in the company which affect the customer's buying decision; its area of interest therefore is often considerably wider than that of other functions.

However, valid though these points are, the conclusion cannot be drawn that marketing is in some way more *important* than the other business functions. Unless *all* functions perform to an acceptable level, then the success of the organization is in jeopardy. Marketing being, so to speak, only one finger on the hand of business functions, it can achieve results solely through working effectively with the other areas of the business.

Relating to other functions

How does marketing contribute to the activities of the other functions? In the first place, it can make a major contribution by *instilling* into the organization a realization of the importance of the customer, thereby *motivating* management and staff from other functions to act accordingly, rather than simply to pay lip service to the idea. Particularly in functions where direct contact with customers is minimal, there is often a tendency to forget that customer satisfaction is the key to success. As a result, standards may slip and slide and a dangerous air of indifference may creep into the organization. Marketing management therefore has the responsibility of liaising with, for example, the production function to ensure that a smooth flow of supply is maintained and that product quality is kept up to the mark.

In the second place, marketing is concerned with mapping out the direction in which the organization must go if it is to achieve its overall objectives. As we have seen, this contribution takes the form of (a) determining and defining the most suitable markets, and (b) ensuring that the organization's resources are used to design, produce and sell a product or range of products in such a way as to maximize favourable buying decisions in those markets. Marketing therefore has a *pathfinding* role to play in relation to the rest of the organization.

What support does marketing itself receive from the other functions? The most important contribution they can make to the success of marketing is to perform in such a way as to meet the market requirements as specified by the marketing function. Thus marketing relies on production for the right products, manufactured to the right quality; on personnel for trained and motivated people; on research and development (R & D) for new product development; and on finance for adequate resources and customer-friendly systems.

Although the overriding goal is clearly that of corporate success, it is perhaps not too difficult to see that en route to this goal there is considerable opportunity for inter-functional conflict. Where conflict does exist, it arises mainly from the different sub-objectives aimed at by the different functions. The production manager, for example, will press for long production runs in order to minimize costs and maximize efficiency; the marketing manager, on the other hand, interested in responding to dynamic market conditions, is likely to argue for a wide range of products and fast change on the production lines.

Another potential source of inter-functional conflict lies in the fact that the activities and achievements of the marketing function can rarely be measured easily. An accountant can measure accurately money spent and money saved; a salesman can have his sales totalled; but a marketing manager is unlikely to be able to find concrete measures for customer-attitude changes or corporate image.

Let us take a closer look at one of the main business functions – finance. Financial management are likely to identify their priorities in the following terms:

> strict rationales for spending
>
> hard-and-fast budgets
>
> pricing to cover costs
>
> tough credit terms
>
> tough collection procedures
>
> standard transactions
>
> few reports.

Managers from the other functions (not least from marketing) may well have other words to describe finance, such as:

money-orientated

penny-pinching

negative attitudes

pessimistic

bureaucratic

suspicious.

Exercise: Take a moment now to reflect on what you have learned so far about the marketing approach. Jot down some notes on how you think other functions might describe marketing; then follow this by noting down some ideas on how the marketing function might describe itself.

It's likely that your first list will include terms like:

over/underselling

extravagant

not cost-conscious

flexible to a fault

loud/brash

flamboyant

ultra-optimistic

uncontrollable.

Your second list, on the other hand, may look something like this:

devising long-term strategy

increasing sales

many models/products to choose from

frequent change

flexible work patterns

good value for money

price incentives.

The solution to such conflicts, of course, generally lies in negotiation and compromise between the different functions. And the likelihood of a successful compromise being reached is much larger if management from the different functions have developed a clear understanding and appreciation of the problems, goals and contributions of their cross-functional colleagues.

Marketing and resources

What kind of financial resources does the marketing function need? First of all, an organization's expenditure on marketing activities must clearly be in scale with the size of the organization's overall financial position. A large firm will need, want and be able to spend more on marketing than will a small local trader. This is obvious. What may be less obvious is the relative importance given to marketing by these two businesses. While the big firm spends more in total on marketing than does the small one, it may actually be spending less in proportion to total funds available (though this is not necessarily the case).

Whatever the funds available, it is important that marketing be allocated as much as can be afforded rather than as little as possible. This means that marketing has to be viewed in its true light as an 'investment' rather than as a 'cost'. It is an investment because money spent on marketing should improve customer satisfaction, which in turn increases customer demand, revenue and, where appropriate, long-term profitability. Good marketing always pays dividends.

In large organizations, the allocation of financial resources is almost universally achieved by annual budgets. These budgets are usually related to organizational departments. This system can create difficulties for marketing because of the way marketing issues cut across departmental boundaries. For instance, budgets connected with distribution will normally be allocated to the transport or distribution department, yet the service provided by this department is a marketing factor. In practice, what tends to happen is that the marketing department is given direct financial responsibility only for those activities which lie totally within the remit of the marketing department staff – such as marketing research and promotion. The department has to rely on influence, political power and organizational awareness of the importance of marketing to achieve its requirements in other areas. A system of this kind creates a good many tensions; it also often means that an organization is not really aware of its full investment in marketing.

Another problem with the annual budgeting system is the very fact that it *is* annual. A good part of marketing expenditure and returns has a far longer cycle than twelve months; image building, for instance, takes years rather than months. Yearly budgets, therefore, unless handled sensitively, can impose false constraints on marketing investment.

By contrast, small firms rarely suffer from annual budgeting and its consequences. Instead, funds tend to be allocated on an *ad hoc* basis. This in turn brings its own problems. One of the main difficulties is that the full financial implications of everything the firm wishes to do are not thought through. This can mean that, when it comes to it, the money needed to pursue a particular marketing plan just isn't available.

Marketing styles

Just as the extent of the marketing activity should be in keeping with the size of the organization, so the *style* of the marketing effort should fit the nature of the organization and its target markets.

Management style can range from the aggressive to the subtle and can be characterized as lavish or frugal, high profile or low profile, and so on. This style is expressed both in the choice of marketing tools and in the way in which the tools selected are used. An 'aggressive' style, for example, will focus on price and promotional/selling activity and is likely to be most effective in market segments where customers show little discrimination between products. The major detergent manufacturers, for example, adopt an aggressive stance when promoting their brands. A stance of this kind, however, is not confined to consumer 'branded' markets. Over the last few years, insurance companies and some investment houses have become increasingly aggressive in their approach, with promises of large sums of money in return for very little outlay.

A 'subtle' style, on the other hand, will focus on product quality and customer service; it is likely to be most effective in market segments where customers are extremely conscious of product differences and are interested in a high level of service. Rolls-Royce and Christian Dior, for example, both emphasize quality, style, reliability and uniqueness.

Marketing styles are often established at a company's inception and are frequently dictated by the market environment. Two examples will illustrate this point. A new company was set up to produce, package and distribute chemicals and detergents for the food and dairy producing industries. Manufacturers, farmers and processors in these industries care little for 'shopping around' and exhibit supplier loyalty. They want the products to be conveniently available and delivered at the cheapest price; provided the price remains good, they will continue to purchase the brand they know.

In this situation, the new company's best policy was to flood the distribution network with its products, offering keenly competitive prices and a variety of promotional gimmicks. Its advertising and selling messages extolled the virtues of its products over those of its competitors. Within a short period of time, the company had established a significant market foothold – but it knew that it had to continue to use an aggressive approach to hold on to its market share.

A new artistic design partnership faced a different situation. Specializing in interior decoration and the refurbishment of period furniture, the partnership was looking for customers from the upper echelons of society. Almost all its marketing therefore was founded on publicity surrounding previous commissions for such customers as the National Trust. New customers came through referral and word-of-mouth.

Checklist

For the marketing function to work in harmony with the rest of the organization, care must be taken to:

analyse the corporate environment and identify any areas of conflict negotiate effective compromises with the functional management involved

provide adequate and appropriate support to the other business functions

ensure that other functions understand clearly what marketing requires of them

have appropriate financial resources allocated to the marketing function

use these resources in the most effective way possible, given the nature of the markets involved.

2 Markets and Customers

5 Defining and Segmenting Markets

What is a market?

The market for any consumer product or service is composed of those people who have a want or need for what the product can give them. The market for watches, for example, comprises people with a need for a portable device which tells the time. In the case of industrial products and services, the market will be composed of organizations which can benefit from use of the product. Thus, the market for ball-bearings comprises organizations which need to ensure the smooth functioning of machinery.

The existence of a commercial market, however, depends on more than the wants and needs of potential customers. A market of this kind can exist only if these potential customers have the funds to fulfil their wants and needs – and if they are willing to use the funds for this purpose.

Exercise: Why might it be important for an organization to define its market? Take a moment to suggest some answers to this question.

Now compare your suggestions with ours. The primary reason for defining a market is to provide the organization with a focus for its activities and plans. It may be helpful – though at first it may not seem so – to think of a market in terms of a race meeting. At these events, there are several different races (markets) which cover different distances and follow different courses. Horses are not entered for every race; instead, each horse runs in the race in which it has the best chance of winning or gaining a high place. (In just the same way, the firm selects the best market opportunity.) Each race requires different skills on the part of the horse-and-jockey team. Long-distance races will require endurance and stamina; the short sprints, speed and acceleration. The extent to which the horse-and-jockey team (the firm) can match the race requirements (market wants and needs) determines the race result.

During the actual race, the competition is direct, in the form of the other runners. But, outside the race, competition is more diffuse, incorporating all horses who could, or might in the future, choose to enter that class of race; other races; other race meetings; and any other events which divert the interest of spectators and racehorse owners. In just the same way, each firm faces both direct and indirect sources of competition. And, unless managers take care to make an accurate identification of the markets which they intend to serve, then they may well overlook the *indirect* sources of competition — that is, firms offering products which meet the same customer *need*, but meet that need in a different way from the first organization.

Let us look at an example of a situation of this kind. If manufacturers of typewriters confine their view of the market to 'people who use typewriters', then they will see the competition as consisting of other firms which produce and sell typewriters. In fact, although any one typewriter manufacturer is quite right to take a keen interest in the fortunes of other typewriter manufacturers, he is quite wrong to ignore the impressive advances made in his market by firms marketing and selling word processors. His mistake has been to define his market too narrowly; and he has made this mistake because he failed to think through the basic wants and needs of those 'people who use typewriters'. Those people don't use typewriters because what they always wanted most in life was a typewriting machine. They use typewriters because, until recently, these machines provided the most efficient way of, for example, producing documents that looked good but were not expensive to supply. (This vital distinction is discussed further in Chapter 11.)

In short, through failing to define his market adequately, our typewriter manufacturer laid himself open to attack from a totally unexpected quarter. He thought that he was playing in one game – but found to his horror that the goalposts had been moved. The skill which he so disastrously lacked was one that is essential to a successful marketer: the ability to make an accurate identification of the relevant customer needs and wants and to define a market in these terms.

This point leads on to another, closely related. Many organizations succumb to the temptation to define their markets in terms of *products* rather than *people*. Thus, a firm may talk of 'the calculator market' rather than 'the market with the need to make accurate calculations quickly and easily'. The reasons for communicating in this kind of shorthand are fairly easy to find. First, more convenient labels can be attached to product-markets (as shown by the calculator example above); and, secondly, product–markets are more distinct and therefore correspondingly more easy to research.

However, there is a major drawback to this approach which easily outweighs the benefits. Basically, it lies in the fact that markets are made up of people, not products. Thinking in terms of products rather than customer needs encourages firms to focus on technological developments in their own particular product area rather than on other developments in the market-place which may completely change the rules of the game. The manufacturers of slide-rules, for example, would have made a costly mistake some time ago had they continued to see their business as being that of producing slide-rules, rather than meeting the need for quick and easy calculations.

Exercise: Can you think of any other examples of a situation where a firm seriously damaged its future prospects through a failure to analyse its market in terms of customer needs?

Segmenting markets

The fact that a substantial number of potential customers have a basic need or want in common does *not* mean that they are all the same and can be treated in the same way. In this context, let us take a closer look at our first example – the need, common to many people, to have available a portable device which tells the time.

Exercise: Take a moment now to jot down some of the different requirements that different groups of people might have for a watch.

You'll probably have included at least some of the following:

> people with limited funds will want a cheap, economical watch
>
> people with poor eyesight will want a watch with a face that is easy to read
>
> children will need a robust timepiece
>
> women who wish to achieve a certain standard of elegance will want a watch that lives up to the rest of their outfit
>
> people involved in sports will want a watch that can also act as a stopwatch
>
> divers will want a truly waterproof timepiece.

In this case, each group of people with different requirements may well represent a *market segment* – that is, a sub-section of the broad market that presents a real marketing opportunity. This marketing opportunity can be located in the fact that the members of the sub-section exhibit very similar requirements which can be met by the same 'total offer' devised by the firm.

The process of dividing markets up into units – in other words, the process of segmentation – is the cornerstone of much marketing activity. Effective market segmentation is about banding customers together into manageable groups, so that the organization can tend to common individual needs on a large enough scale to be both profitable to the organization and satisfactory to the customers.

Why bother with segmentation?

There are several excellent reasons for seeking to achieve a sensibly segmented market.

The first reason relates back to the point made very early on in this book. Marketing, you will remember, is primarily about *matching* the organization's resources with the customers' needs. The main focus of a process of market segmentation is to identify people (or organizations) who have similar requirements to each other – but who differ in these requirements from the general market profile. If the organization separates out these people as a distinct market segment, then this process enables it to:

> develop offers that match customer requirements more accurately
>
> focus its marketing activity on those customers whose requirements are most compatible with the organization's resources.

The second advantage of a segmented market is that the organization can develop more sharply focused marketing strategies; in other words, the marketing planning process can be based on a detailed knowledge and understanding of individual market segments.

What are the alternatives to a segmented marketing approach? At one extreme, the organization can treat the whole market as having the same requirements; at the other, it can seek to treat each customer separately and individually. Neither approach has usually much to commend it, in either practical or theoretical terms. While many firms might *wish* that all customers were the same and wanted the same benefits, this wish is rarely granted. At the other extreme, marketing to individual customers rarely makes economic sense.

The skill of segmentation

Any description of a market segment must hold the answers to the following questions:

What do the customers want?

Who are the customers who want these things?

Indeed, it is a cardinal rule of segmentation that markets are segmented by customer needs and wants, not by the products they buy.

Considerable skill is involved in choosing the best basis for segmentation. One or more of the following methods are often employed in consumer markets.

1. Benefit segmentation

Here, the market is segmented on the basis of the benefit sought by the customer. Thus, for example, banks promote high-interest deposit accounts to people who are more interested in accumulating capital than in being assured of easy access to their savings. Direct and customer-orientated, this approach is often very effective. The main problem is that benefits are not always easily identified – and customers may not be able to describe exactly what it is they want.

2. Demographic segmentation

A very common approach, demographic segmentation involves categorizing markets in terms of age, sex, education, income, marital status and class. In your reading elsewhere, you may well have come across references to the socio-economic groupings, A, B, C1, C2, D and E. What exactly do these letters indicate about the status of people categorized in this way? The groupings take the following form:

A: upper middle-class – for example, the highest ranks of managers, administrators and professional people

B: middle-class – for example, middle-ranking managers, administrators and professional people

C1: lower middle-class – for example, supervisors, clerks, junior managers, administrators and professional people

C2: skilled working-class – for example, skilled manual workers

D: working-class – for example, semi- and unskilled manual workers

E: subsistence level – for example, state pensioners and casual, lowest-grade workers.

This scheme is the most widely used classification – although it has attracted extensive criticism as being unrepresentative of current socio-economic patterns.

The success of demographic segmentation lies in the fact that variables such as class and age do indeed often correlate closely with purchase behaviour. However, there is a drawback: this method tends to shed light only on purchase behaviour with regard to *types* of products; it provides little information on how and why the different segments select particular versions or brands of a product type.

3. Psychographic or life-style segmentation

This method uses a number of variables to segment markets according to the way people live their lives. Demographic factors are usually included, along with information on activities, interests, opinions, personality and social role. Perhaps the most well-known system of psychographic segmentation is that developed by SRI International (formerly the Stanford Research Institute). Known as VALS, this system defines nine basic segments:

> belongers (patriotic, stable, sentimental traditionalists who are content with their lives)
>
> achievers (prosperous, self-assured, middle-aged materialists)
>
> emulators (ambitious young adults trying to break into the system)
>
> I-am-me group (impulsive, experimental, a bit narcissistic)
>
> experiential (people-orientated, inner growth directed)
>
> societally conscious (mature, successful, mission-orientated people who like causes)

survivors (the old and poor with little optimism about the future)

sustainers (resentful of their condition and trying to make ends meet)

integrated (psychologically mature, balanced and self-fulfilling).

4. *Usage segmentation*

Analysis of patterns of usage of the product can sometimes reveal the existence of discrete segments. Heavy users, for instance, may show different buying behaviour from light users.

5. *Geographic segmentation*

This approach highlights the importance of regional factors in influencing buying behaviour. Customers in the same geographic regions may be found to share common traits and patterns. This kind of segmentation can be extended to include type of areas (urban, rural, lowland, highland, for example) as well as specific regions. Thus, rural customers may be found to want a mail order or delivery service, while urban dwellers might prefer to visit shops.

In fact, segmentation often incorporates elements of each of these approaches. The result is that firms may define market segments in terms of demographic and life-style characteristics as well as location, usage patterns and benefit requirements. Comprehensive market segment profiles of this kind facilitate targeted marketing.

Segmenting industrial markets

Several of the factors described above – benefit, geographic and usage variables, for example – are also relevant in segmenting industrial markets. However, other types of factor are also involved in such markets. These include:

1. *the type of industry served.* Many industrial products – such as ball-bearings – can be sold into a variety of indus-

tries and organizations. Each of these customer groups is likely to present different needs and problems. Choosing which group to concentrate on is therefore a natural first step for the supplier interested in market segmentation.

2. *the level of customer service required.* Some industrial customers will wish to buy in bulk; others will prefer to place individual orders. Some may insist on immediate delivery; others will be prepared to wait. Some may require a high level of after-sales service; others will prefer to carry out in-house servicing. The supplier may well find it useful to carry out a segmentation exercise on the basis of differences of this kind.

Choosing the basis for segmentation

There is no standard answer to the question of how the organization can choose the most appropriate basis of segmentation. In practice, many firms use one or more of the following approaches:

1. *intuition and experience.* Experienced managers often segment their markets by 'feel'. This approach is often successful; but risk is reduced if such intuition is backed up by objective information and evidence.
2. *trial and error.*
3. *research on customers.* Research can cover attitudes, opinions, requirements, usage patterns and character-istics in an attempt to reveal significant similarities.

The last approach is the one most likely to lead to an effective segmentation exercise. However, even here, risks are involved. Research results invariably demand interpretation; and many man-agers experience an overwhelming temptation to interpret results according to their pet theories about the market, along with its needs and wants.

When is a segment a real segment?

A simple procedure can help managers check the validity of their market segments.

First of all, they need to be guided by two golden rules:

1. customers should be segmented by their needs and wants, not by the product they buy.
2. *all* customers should be grouped in this way, not just the organization's own customers.

Secondly, managers should check through the following five questions. If they can answer 'yes' to each one, then their segmentation strategy is sound.

> Are the needs that differentiate the customer groups genuinely different and easily discernible?
>
> Are the customers in one segment broadly similar in behaviour?
>
> Are the benefits we have chosen to use to describe a particular segment really relevant to the choice the customer makes when making buying decisions?
>
> Is each segment of sufficient size to yield an adequate return on effort?
>
> Can potential customers in each segment be readily identified and reached?

Exercise: Think of a situation where your own organization, or an organization well known to you, carried out a market segmentation exercise. Was the exercise successful? If so, describe the factors that contributed to its success. If the segmentation did not prove successful, try to identify the reasons for its failure. Lastly, put that segmentation strategy to the test described above. How did it stand up to this analysis? How might the segmentation have been improved?

What next?

Having first defined its overall market and then gone on to identify a number of market segments within that market, an organization does not usually proceed to assail all the customer groups identified. Instead, it chooses particular market segments or niches (that is, parts of a segment) and targets those for further marketing attention. The segments selected are known as 'target markets'. The process of analysing market opportunities in order to select the most appropriate is an issue taken up again in Chapters 8 and 10.

Checklist

In assessing the markets which it intends to serve, an organization should:

define its market in terms of customer *wants* and *needs*

seek to achieve a sensible segmentation of that market

select the most appropriate basis of segmentation, having examined:
   benefit segmentation
   demographic segmentation
   psychographic segmentation
   usage segmentation
   geographic segmentation
   the methods of segmenting industrial markets

use the basic criteria of successful segmentation to check that its segments are valid.

6 Identifying the Customers

What's in a name?

Exercise: (1) Are 'customer' and 'consumer' just different words to describe the same person? (2) What about an 'end user' – is this just the same person under yet another guise? (3) And does it all matter anyway? Take a moment now to decide your answers to these three questions.

The short answers we would suggest are, respectively:
1. 'Sometimes, and sometimes not'
2. 'Not usually'
3. 'Yes'.

However, since these answers are rather uninformative, let's examine the issues involved in rather more detail.

First of all, it is important to grasp the fact that, in a sense, it is irrelevant whether the 'customer' and 'consumer' *are* the same person. The point of crucial importance is that the words 'customer' and 'consumer' refer to quite different *roles* in the buying process; and, unless marketers have clearly identified these different roles in their markets, they have very little chance of achieving marketing success. Customers and consumers *are* different – and different in important ways. Even if, in particular circumstances, customer and consumer are represented by the same person, the marketer must take care to respond to the needs implicit in the two different roles.

So, what *are* these roles and what needs do they represent? Let's start with customers.

Customers

Customers are the people who do the buying, who actually guarantee payment for the products or services on offer. Different customers will have different purposes in mind when they buy. For example, industrial customers may buy in order to:

> use the product to make another product (as in the use of timber to make wood-pulp)

> use or consume the product in the course of their business (as in the use of office stationery)

> sell the product on to another business (as in selling paper to an office supplies intermediary)

> sell the product to a final end user (as in selling paper to an office manager).

Customers who are *not* industrial customers – that is, customers who are not buying on behalf of an organization – may buy in order to:

> use or consume the product (as, for example, in the use of cooking oil in the preparation of a meal or in buying a snack to eat)

> give to another person (a Christmas present, for example)

> use the product to satisfy somebody else's needs (as in the case of a mother buying food for her family).

As these examples make clear, both in industrial and non-industrial situations, customers often act as *buying agents* for other people. That is to say, customers always have the responsibility of selecting and purchasing goods; in many cases, however, they may assume this responsibility with other people's interests in mind. The wise marketer will never forget this fact – and will ensure that his or her organization's offering is geared to the full range of the customer's concerns.

Consumers

The consumer is the person who actually consumes or uses the product. This person may also have the role of customer, but this is by no means invariably the case.

Consumers are important in marketing because, as we shall see later in this chapter, they can exert considerable influence over the buying decision made by the customer. For the moment, this point may be illustrated by an everyday example from consumer marketing: which mother (customer) can long withstand her children's (consumer) demands to eat certain types of convenience food?

A word of warning. The term 'consumer' is not only used in the way described above. It is also used in marketing to refer to individuals acting in a private capacity – hence the phrase, 'consumer markets'. Once you are aware of this dual usage, you will usually find it fairly straightforward to determine how the term is being used in any given context.

End users

The role of 'end user' closely resembles that of 'consumer'. The term is most commonly used:

(a) in industrial markets (for example, when fork-lift trucks are the product involved, reference is made to 'end users' rather than to 'consumers')

(b) in markets where the product in question is being used rather than consumed (for example, computer markets and services such as air travel)

(c) to refer to the last and 'consuming' member of a distribution chain. Wholesalers and retailers, for instance, are neither end users nor consumers of the products they buy and sell; but the final purchaser usually is one of these.

Exercise: Think of a product or service familiar to you. For this product, who are (a) the customers, (b) the consumers, (c) (if appropriate) the end users? Does the firm supplying the product take this distinction into account in its marketing? If so, how does it do this? If not, how might the firm usefully address this distinction?

Markets and customers

Markets are made up of customers – both existing customers and potential customers. When a manufacturer of word processors contemplates his potential market, for example, he includes in his calculations both the number of people currently using word processors and the number that he anticipates could benefit from the use of such machines. As far as the individual firm is concerned, its *existing customers* are those people with whom it is already doing business; its *potential customers* are those people with whom it believes it *could* do business if it gets its selling messages right.

Market share is represented by the proportion of total sales to a market achieved by an individual firm. Thus, the annual market for, say, new telephone answering machines may be around one million units a year; Company A sells 100,000 units a year; therefore its market share is 10 per cent. As in this example, current market share is measured by sales to *existing* customers. Predictions about future market share usually incorporate sales to *potential* customers as well.

Market share figures are frequently quoted; but they are notoriously unreliable and often have little meaning. Their notoriety resides in the fact that the market shares quoted by firms in any one market rarely add up to 100 per cent; and the value of these figures to marketing management is frequently further restricted by the use of unimaginative and inappropriate product–markets as the basis for calculation.

There is another category of customer, however, that is rather more difficult to identify. This is the *lost* or *past* customer. When is a customer 'lost' to an organization? In other words, how long ago does a customer have to have bought in order to qualify still as an 'existing customer'? The answer to this depends on the type of product and type of industry involved.

Generally, a firm's customer records will show the frequency and quantity of individual customers' purchases. Any change in buying patterns of this kind should be automatically followed up by the firm. The customers concerned will obviously have explanations of their own for the change, and these should be given careful attention. However, the shrewd marketer will also make an appraisal of:

> competitor activity (such as special promotions and improved service)
>
> customer standing and performance relative to the market
>
> any neglect on the part of the firm itself.

In addition to this detailed analysis of the behaviour of individual customers, the marketer will probably also find it useful to undertake an on-going appraisal of the total customer profile. In this way, he or she can identify any general movements or trends and assess the significance of any shifts in the customer base.

The decision-making unit

Sometimes individual customers do make autonomous buying decisions. Perhaps more often, however, the customer acts as a buying agent and is influenced in his or her buying decisions by one or more interested others. Marketing shorthand describes a scenario of this kind as a decision-making unit (DMU). Thus, where customers are buying on behalf of others (the consumers), these others become part of the whole decision-making unit for purchase. It is essential that marketers identify and take account of all members of the DMUs typically found in their market.

The various people in any DMU will have different roles in the buying process. They will also have different interests and concerns. The successful marketer will be prepared to research these different interests and respond to them with appropriate messages.

Let us look at some examples of DMUs in operation. First of all, consider the preparation for a decision on a family holiday. Research findings suggest that members of the family tend to fall into the following roles within the household DMU:

1. The *wife* collects the holiday brochures. Bearing in mind the budget available and the different interests of members of the family, she then makes a preliminary selection of a range of holidays.

2. The *husband* has the power of veto. He tends to indicate where he does *not* want to go on holiday and the type of holiday he does *not* want. He may see no objection to several of the holidays selected by his wife.

3. The *children* usually have no direct say in the final decision. However, they almost invariably exert a great deal of influence on what is decided. They may, for example, point out the advantages and disadvantages of the different holidays in terms of their own activities and preferences; and they are not likely to be slow in suggesting that if *their* preferences are followed, then their parents will be able to look forward to a modicum of peace and quiet on holiday.

In this example, all members of the family are consumers or end users. But who are the customers? Depending on who makes the actual purchase, it may be the husband, the wife or both.

Our second example concerns the decision to buy a new word processor for an office. Here, the line-up is likely to be as follows:

1. The *line manager* will want to know whether the machine is reliable and whether it will enable its operator to produce the required results.

2. The *office equipment manager* also will want to know whether the machine is reliable. In addition, he or she will be interested in finding out whether it is compatible with other word processors and whether its price is comparable with that of similar machines.

3. The *user/operator* will want to know whether the machine looks and feels 'right'. This member of the DMU does not usually have a formal say in the final buying decision. However, many large firms have found that operators who are unhappy with the choice of system made for them subsequently make their discontent felt by rising less than enthusiastically to the challenges posed by the new equipment. As a result, user/operators are now often given the power of veto on the final decision.

There may well be another, shadowy, member of this DMU – the person who made the initial collection of information on the various word processing systems available and passed this information on to the others. This person decides what information about which systems is relevant and worth consideration. This very process of selection exerts considerable, albeit indirect, influence on the final buying decision.

In commercial situations there are, on average, four people involved in any significant buying decision. Each one of these people needs to be persuaded of the benefits that apply to him or her; and each person may be reached only through an appropriate channel of communication. When choosing which communication channels to use (a subject to be discussed further in Chapters 21 and 22) the marketer should bear these needs constantly in mind.

Research has also shown that within most DMUs there are the following roles:

> the information collector
>
> the final decider
>
> the pusher (that is, the person who wants the decision made but hasn't the power to make it)
>
> the user/consumer
>
> the financier.

Needless to say, one person may have more than one role within the DMU (for instance, a person may be both the pusher and the end user); and one role may be shared by two or more DMU members (for instance, more than one person may collect information or push for a decision).

In many markets today, the trend is towards more complicated DMUs. An essential marketing skill therefore lies in our ability to identify at an early stage the allocation of real decision-making power – and to direct appropriate messages to each of the people

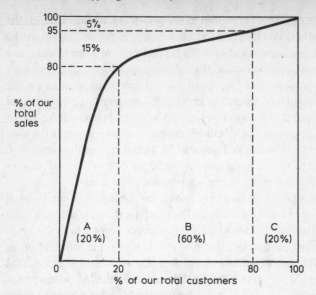

Figure 6.1.   The 80/20 rule or Pareto effect

concerned. Unless this challenge is successfully met, the marketer will waste time and resources in appealing in the wrong way to the wrong people.

The 80/20 rule

Who are an organization's most important customers? The answer in most cases will be either 'those customers who buy our product most frequently and most intensively' or 'those customers who contribute most to our profit'.

In either case, in whatever market concerns them, marketers are likely to come across a phenomenon known as the '80/20 rule' or the 'Pareto effect'. This is just shorthand for the observed fact that in most markets a comparatively small number of customers account for (a) most of the sales, and (b) most of the profit. It should be noted, however, that it is by no means always the case that the *same* customers generate both most sales *and* most profit.

In many markets, analysis of the relationship between customers and sales can direct attention to the group of customers which the organization, knowingly or unknowingly, is depending on for its prosperity. Figure 6.1 shows the typical ratio of sales to customer groups found in the Pareto effect. An organization's customers have here been classed as 'A', 'B' or 'C' customers, depending on the proportion of total sales they represent. Representing 20 per cent of the total number of customers, the 'A' customers account for 80 per cent of total sales. The 'B' customers make up 60 per cent of the total number of customers and account for 15 per cent of the total sales; while the 'C' customers, representing 20 per cent of the total number of customers, account for only 5 per cent of total sales.

The 80/20 rule can be a very useful tool for the marketer, helping him or her to focus attention on the customers who contribute most to the business. Having established which customers form the 'critical mass' of the market, the marketer can use this information as a basis for segmentation and for deciding which type of potential customers to seek out in future. For example, the 'A' category customers might be visited more frequently by sales representatives than the 'C' category customers. Similarly, 'A' category customers' demands and requirements might receive priority in periods of short supply.

A word of caution in managing customers according to the 80/20 rule. Remember that the constant state of flux in the market-place will mean that some 'A' category customers may be declining in importance while some 'B' or 'C' category customers may be increasing in importance – and might represent future 'A' category customers if they are given the right service and attention. Another consideration will be demand fluctuations, such as seasonal variations; 'A' category customers in the summer, for instance, could well become 'C' category customers during the winter.

Checklist

Once target markets have been selected, the organization should:

identify, as relevant, its customers, consumers and end users assess the extent of its potential market as well as its existing market

identify the main DMUs to be found in its market

analyse what benefits are relevant to each of the members of the DMU

analyse its market in terms of the 80/20 rule.

7 The What, How and Why of Buying

Who cares about buying behaviour?

For the marketer, knowledge of how customers make buying decisions is not a luxury; it is essential information. Marketers need to understand buyer behaviour in order both to establish cause–effect relationships in the market-place and to optimize the allocation of marketing resources in such areas as advertising, selling, pricing and customer service.

Exercise: Take a moment to jot down what you think might be covered by that phrase 'buyer behaviour'.

Now compare your notes with our suggestions. Analysing buyer behaviour includes finding out about:

>which customers are in the market for a particular product
>
>what these customers want
>
>how they buy
>
>how frequently they purchase the product
>
>how frequently they use the product
>
>how satisfied they are with it
>
>how they learn about the different products available in the area of interest
>
>how they choose between makes or brands
>
>how they choose between sources of supply

to what extent customers are affected by the image of the organization and its advertising messages.

As you will know from your own experience as a customer, there is no set pattern for buying behaviour. There are certain differences, of course, between different types of customer (between industrial customers, say, and those buying fast-moving consumer goods); but, equally, individual customers in these groups may behave differently from one another. Marketers for any product or service have no choice but to make a careful study of the behaviour exhibited by the different groups that are of interest to them. Fortunately, there are some guidelines to help them in this difficult but necessary task.

Influences on buying behaviour

The behaviour of a buyer varies according to a whole host of factors. These include:

whether or not the purchase is being made in an area where the customer has knowledge and expertise and consequently feels comfortable

whether or not the product or service being acquired holds an emotional significance for the customer

whether the purchase is a major one, representing considerable expenditure, or a minor one, involving small outlay. Where the purchase is a major one, most customers will devote more time to weighing up the options

whether the purchase is a new one to the customer or a repeat purchase. As we shall see later in this chapter, new purchases are usually given more conscious thought and attention than are repeat purchases.

The *context* of the buying decision is also likely to be an important influence on how the customer goes about making his or her decision. If, for example, a person is making a buying decision in his or her role as a buyer for an organization, then that decision is

likely to be approached rather differently from a purchase made by
the same person in a supermarket at the weekend.

Exercise: Note down some of the characteristics which you think
may distinguish 'industrial' or 'organizational' buyers
from 'consumers'. (In this context, 'consumers' are private
individuals buying on their own account.)

The *traditional* wisdom in marketing has it that industrial buyers
and consumers are creatures cut from a very different cloth. Industrial buyers, it is said, are entirely 'rational' in their decisions, weighing up with cold logic the pros and cons of the various options on
offer. Consumers, on the other hand, are allegedly flighty buyers,
always ready to be affected in their decisions by a change in the
weather or some other extraneous factor. In fact, more recent
research has shown that although there *are* differences between
these two types of buyer, the differences are neither as extensive nor
as profound as had previously been supposed. The main differences
are associated with the following factors:

> industrial buying decisions tend to involve more formal-
> ized and methodical deliberations

> the decision-making units in industrial purchasing tend
> to be complicated and involve a good many people; con-
> sumer DMUs are more frequently based on the household
> or family unit.

These differences apart, the two types of buyer can be seen to share
a good many characteristics. Both groups, for example, make buying
decisions according to the role assigned to them; both are subject to
the influence of other members of a DMU; and both are affected by
personal, emotional factors. Industrial buyers, it appears, are human
too . . .

Buy phases

The buying process has been broken down into a standard set of five phases:

1. A problem/need/want is recognized. Needs often emerge in the form of a problem which needs a solution. In industrial markets, for example, the problem may involve the expansion of production, the requirement to reduce manufacturing costs, dissatisfaction with the service provided by current suppliers, and so on. Wants and needs may be specific or vague. For example, a consumer may be specific about wanting a product to eat or wear; or may have a need for change, excitement or adventure but have no specific product in mind.

2. The requirement is identified. The buyer consults with others to determine what types of product and/or services may satisfy the need.

3. A search for alternative solutions is made. The buyer seeks information about various products which may satisfy his or her needs.

4. Options are evaluated. This stage will be discussed in greater detail later in the chapter. Suffice it to say here that buyers perceive different risks in different purchase situations. These risks relate both to uncertainty about how the product will perform and to the consequences which might arise from the purchase. For example, the housewife's choice puts at risk both her housekeeping money and the approval or otherwise of her family. The industrial buyer's choice risks the dissatisfaction of the production manager with the supplies ordered – and may endanger his or her own job as a professional purchasing officer.

5. A decision is made.
The kind of methodical approach implicit in the buy phases can be described as 'conscious' or 'deliberate' buying. This kind of buying tends to predominate when:

the purchase is a major one and/or is undertaken infrequently. Buying a house or a new item of industrial plant would fall into this category

the purchase is 'new' to the customer – that is, being made by him or her for the first time

there has been dissatisfaction with a previous purchase

there is a need to conform to rules or norms (as, for example, in organizational buying)

the personality of the buyer is such that this approach is an attractive and natural one.

With this type of buying, the customer's goals tend to be displayed fairly clearly. However, even when purchase goals are not so obvious, it should be borne in mind that *all* buyers have goals and are guided by these as well as by wants and beliefs.

Generally speaking, it seems that the buy phases described above are more often followed in a systematic way by industrial buyers than by consumers. Even in industrial buying, however, not all the phases may apply for each purchase decision. Nevertheless, this categorization offers a useful starting point and initial framework for analysing buyer behaviour.

Type of buying situation

We have already referred to the importance of identifying whether the purchase being made is 'new' to the customer or whether the purchase is a 'familiar' one.

Exercise: Can you think of a recent situation where you made a 'new buy' – that is, found yourself in a position where you felt the need for a product hitherto unfamiliar to you? (For example, perhaps you decided to buy a computer, house, gardening tools or the services of an accountant for the first time.) How did you go about choosing which product to buy?

You'll probably have noted down that you started from scratch in your hunt for information and advice. You realized that your past experience of purchasing wasn't particularly helpful in this case and that you had to find some other basis on which to build useful criteria for evaluation.

Exercise: Now think of a situation where your basic need was a familiar one but differed in one or two important respects from your previous experience. (Our example here could be the need for a new filing cabinet which offered both more storage space than the old one and an 'easier to use' design.) How did you go about choosing which product to buy?

Here, you'll probably have answered that you had a much clearer idea of the factors involved in your purchase decision. You didn't need to go back to the beginning of the buying process; all you wanted was some additional information to help you ensure that your purchase would fulfil the new needs you had identified. In marketing jargon, this type of buying situation is known as a 'modified rebuy'.

Exercise: Finally, think of a situation in which you needed to purchase a product – but, since nothing had changed in your circumstances and you had made the same type of purchase before, you knew exactly which product would fit the bill. How did you approach this buying decision?

Your answer here is probably that you didn't bother about exploring options – you went out and bought a simple replacement for the original product. In marketing jargon, this type of buying situation is known as a 'straight rebuy'.

Take a moment now to look at Table 7.1 which summarizes these different buying situations and their implications for buying behaviour.

TABLE 7.1. *Distinguishing characteristics of buying situations*

Type of buying situation	Newness of the problem	Experience and information requirements	Consideration of buying alternatives
New buy	Problem or requirement is new to buying decision-makers	Past experience is not considered relevant, much information required	Buying alternatives not known All solutions considered are new
Modified rebuy	Problem or requirement is not new but is somewhat different from previous similar situations	Past experience relevant, but more information required before making decision	New alternative solutions, whether or not known, will be considered before making buying decision
Straight rebuy	Continuing or recurring requirement	Past experience considered sufficient to make buying decision, with little or no additional information required	Alternative solutions may be known but are not given serious consideration

So, what implications do these findings hold for marketers? Quite simply – but crucially – they mean that marketers must make every effort to adapt their 'total offer' to meet the different needs presented. In a 'new buy' situation, for example, the marketer must take care, through appropriate advertising and selling messages, to offer sufficient reassurance and support to overcome the hesitation and worry felt by the buyer. For a 'modified rebuy', the marketer must emphasize new features and benefits; and in a 'straight rebuy', the message is likely to be 'still the best you can buy'.

Evaluative criteria

Once the search has been made for alternative solutions to a buying problem (buy phase 3), options will be evaluated (buy phase 4). Evaluation is usually based on the following criteria:

the success of the product in fulfilling its basic use func-

tion (a watch, for example, may be judged in terms of its
accuracy in keeping time)

the success of the product in living up to the additional
promises made for it (with a 'waterproof' watch, for
example, divers will soon be able to judge just how well
the timepiece takes the underwater strain)

These criteria are examined in greater detail below.

Evaluation of basic use

Several approaches may be used in evaluation of this kind. They
include:

1. technical performance criteria.   Here, products are assessed
according to (a) what they do, and (b) how well they do it. A vacuum
cleaner, for example, could be evaluated in the following terms: 'it
lifts more dust more quickly and is easier to handle'.

2. official standards.   Where British Safety Standards exist, a
product may be judged in terms of whether or not it meets these
standards.

Evaluation of additional benefits

Again, several approaches may be taken, including:

1. personal issues.   *Status* may be an important issue in a purchase
decision. A fountain pen, for example, may be valued primarily as a
status symbol. *Fashion* too may be important, as when an important
influence in choice is whether the item chosen will give the individual a heightened sense of being 'fashionable' or 'forward thinking'.
The importance of status and fashion is not confined to consumer
buying – these factors are also relevant in industrial buying.

2. economic issues.   The important factors here are likely to
include: price; cost per unit; value for money; and the opportunity
costs involved in buying or not buying the product.

3. reference to the experience/opinions of other people.   When buying a new product or buying in an area where he or she has limited knowledge, the purchaser may turn to other people's experience in an attempt to reduce the uncertainty surrounding the purchase. This approach, known as 'reference behaviour', may involve:

> imitating those perceived as having more experience in the area. Thus, a purchaser may choose Brand X word processor on the grounds that his friend Bill knows all about computers and he, Bill, always goes for Brand X

> seeking advice. This may come from promotional brochures and sales literature as well as from friends and colleagues

> paying particular attention to the 'name' of the supplier/ producer. Choosing a product with a well-known brand name from a reputable manufacturer is often seen as a way of reducing risk. Industrial buyers may well put a great deal of stress on the reputation of the supplier for meeting orders satisfactorily

> making a trial purchase. Here, the purchaser will, if possible, place an initial small order so that he or she can judge the quality of the product.

4. guarantees and refund offers available.   The knowledge that, if something goes wrong with the product, compensation or replacement will be available sometimes tips the balance in the purchasing decision.

Selection

Once buyers have evaluated the options available to them, they normally proceed to selecting the product they consider most appropriate to their needs. This selection usually involves some kind of 'trade-off', simply because few products can supply customers with *everything* they would like. Some marketers have even used this point to their advantage. One small business, for example, used to display a card in its premises reading:

> 'Customers always want the cheapest price, the best qual-
> ity and the fastest delivery time. We can always provide
> two of the above, but never all three.'

The final selection of the product is a process still shrouded in some mystery. No theory has yet offered an adequate explanation as to exactly how the different factors involved in the decision are weighed against one another. The procedures are often fairly explicit in industrial buying where weighting models and charts may be used; but, even here, in practice the procedures are often 'adjusted' to provide the answer that the buyer wants to hear.

Habit buying

The kind of buying that we have been concentrating on so far involves a conscious, deliberate process of choice. However, this is by no means the only pattern of buying to be found in the market-place. *Habit buying* is one common alternative.

Habits save time and effort. They are based on previous experience. 'Habit buying' therefore means that after the first few purchases of a particular item, the buyer hardly needs to make a 'conscious' buying decision. Only a change in his or her needs, or new information about an alternative product, is likely to change the established pattern of behaviour.

Obviously, patterns of this kind are very attractive to the supplier. However, marketers can too easily mistake habit buying for loyalty to a particular brand or product; and such a mistake can leave the supplier very vulnerable to the competition. The central ingredient of habit is inertia, a quality quite different from the more positive 'loyalty'. While habit buying can produce results very similar to loyalty buying in the short term, its long-term prospects are usually much less favourable. Some of the high street banks, for example, believed that they had a solid mass of 'loyal' customers; but when the building societies began to offer products more than competitive with those offered by the banks, many 'loyal' customers deserted the banks in droves. It became clear that what had been presumed to be 'loyalty' was actually nothing more than inertia and a vague feeling that 'there was nothing better available'.

Picking

As the term suggests, *picking* involves making a more or less random selection of a product, brand or make. This pattern of buying predominates in situations where:

there is little perceived difference between brands

the value of the transaction is not great.

Some supermarket shopping is of this type; and it is for this reason that pack design and the positioning of the product in the store are so important. A product is much more likely to be 'picked' if it is eye-catchingly packaged and prominently displayed. Confectionery manufacturers have this fact in mind when they press for their chocolate bars and sweets to be displayed in the check-out area of supermarkets.

Picking can also be found in catalogue shopping. For example, a clerical officer may need a batch of new files and see that a particular catalogue offers files of the right size. Not particularly concerned about the type of file needed, he proceeds to 'pick' rather than 'choose' them from the catalogue.

Decisions based on personal taste

An important factor in buying behaviour, this is usually beyond even the best marketer's reach. Why, for instance, do you like coffee while I prefer tea? Neither of us can really explain it, apart from saying that each of us prefers one taste to the other.

When personal taste is involved, the buyer usually chooses on an emotional basis rather than as a result of deliberation. However, this is by no means always the case: customers may *not* in fact buy the preferred option. Consider, for example, a situation where a person *prefers* full cream milk to skimmed milk, but actually *buys* the skimmed variety on the grounds that it will do less damage to his or her diet.

Post-purchase assessment

Once the buying decision has been taken and the product has been put to use (or consumed), the transaction will be subject to post-purchase assessment. Such assessment ranges from an instant 'I liked that' about a chocolate bar to a long-term evaluation of a car or a house. Phrases like 'that was a good buy' or 'that was a waste of money' make up the colloquial expressions of such evaluation.

Marketers should not ignore the importance of this stage of buying behaviour. If they want the customer to return (as most marketers do), then they must ensure that post-purchase evaluation reinforces the buying decision made. One way of doing this is to use 'reinforcement' advertising. This is important in both the industrial and consumer markets. The woman who has just bought a BMW and the man who has just installed a new computer system in his office both want to be told what excellent choices they have made.

The need to reassure and encourage purchasers *after* purchase is highlighted by the implications of a widely accepted psychological theory known as 'cognitive dissonance'. This theory suggests that whenever an individual makes a decision to purchase, he or she will later suffer from doubts and anxieties about the selection made. This is because, where the choice has been between attractive alternatives, the individual knows that the alternatives *not* selected had certain *desirable* features while the item selected usually possesses some *undesirable* features which must now be accepted. When this 'dissonance' exists, an individual will attempt to reduce it by such methods as playing down or denying the importance of the negative features of the purchase and/or enhancing the positive elements. This behaviour is called 'dissonance reduction'.

Clearly, the sensible marketer will use these findings as an incentive to step up his or her efforts to reassure customers that they have made the best choice.

Non-purchase

It is by no means unusual to find that a purchase decision seems very likely – but, in the end, fails to materialize. There can be several reasons for this, including:

the discovery by an industrial buyer that the product most appropriate to his or her needs is manufactured by an overseas company – but the employing organization's policy is to buy British

the refusal by a consumer to buy an otherwise satisfactory product as a protest against the government policies of the country of origin of the product (South African Cape fruit, for example, is widely rejected on these grounds)

the influence of other people on the consumer's purchasing decision (parents, for example, may persuade a teenager not to buy a much coveted motorcycle)

consumer hesitation due to lack of time, expertise or motivation.

Checklist

In exploring how its customers make buying decisions, the organization must:

identify what influences on buying behaviour are particularly important in its markets

determine whether and how its customers pass through 'buy phases'

identify the types of buying situation it is likely to confront in its marketing

understand the evaluative criteria used by its customers

determine whether – or in what proportion – (a) conscious, deliberate buying, (b) habit buying, (c) picking, or (d) decisions based on personal taste exist in its markets

pay adequate attention to the post-purchase stage

analyse why the decision is made *not* to purchase.

8 Analysing Market Opportunities

When is a market opportunity a real market opportunity?

Successful marketing is rather like hitting a moving target. Markets are always changing; trends are unpredictable and, while new opportunities arise, others die. It is because of this uncertainty that we need to know and understand as much as we can about customers and markets. Only in this way can market trends, and hence market opportunities, be anticipated with any confidence.

But not all opportunities which may be identified in a market-place are real market opportunities as far as an individual business is concerned. The only *real* market opportunities are those which a business can successfully exploit – in other words, those opportunities which best match the capabilities and circumstances of the firm.

Think back for a moment to Part One. Do you remember the point being made that marketing is all about using resources to develop offers which meet market wants and needs?

Where are we now?

Internal analysis

The process of analysing market opportunities is usually best begun at home through an *internal analysis*. 'Know thyself' is an important maxim in marketing as well as in other areas of business and life. Until an organization has a clear idea of its current marketing position, it is unlikely to be able to make any realistic assessment of future prospects in the market-place.

Although the aim is a marketing appraisal of a business, this does not mean that the internal analysis is confined to the directly market-related areas of operation. Rather, this type of analysis involves looking at every aspect of the business from the perspective of its effect on marketing. Thus, reviews of financial resources, plant, production capacities, workforce skills and the like are essential, since these factors can determine just what an organization can and cannot do.

A useful framework for undertaking this *internal analysis* is to divide the task into four areas:

1. **Customers:** numbers, types, sizes and importance, requirements, products purchased, etc.

2. **Sales:**   volume, value, by market segment, by product, market share, etc.

3. **Marketing activities:**   market research, new product development, product range and positioning, prices and discounts, promotional activities, selling methods, distribution channels, customer service, etc.

4. **Other factors:**   production capacity, workforce and management skills, capital, corporate goals and policy, finance, etc.

What about the rest of the world?
External analysis

Once an objective assessment of these areas has been made, the organization is in a much better position to begin considering how it stands *vis-à-vis* its competitors and markets. However, before the complete picture can be gained, a thorough *external analysis* must be carried out.

As we saw in Chapter 3, analysis of the marketing environment is of great importance in laying the groundwork for marketing policies. The external analysis undertaken by the individual organization represents its attempt to identify the main features of the environment in which it intends to operate. Environmental factors have an enormous impact on customer requirements and buying behaviour. An understanding of environmental influences on the market-place is therefore very important – especially as these influences represent those elements of the marketing picture over which a business has no control.

For appraisal purposes, the environment can be usefully divided into six areas: legal and political; economic; cultural and social; technological; institutional; and competition. There is considerable overlap between the categories; however, this should not be seen as a problem. It simply means that the same event may fit conveniently in several places.

A simple guide to what each category means is provided by the following questions. Note, however, that these questions are merely illustrative. They are by no means exhaustive nor will all be relevant in every situation.

1. Legal and political:

What are the effects of existing legislation?

What new legislation will become effective?

What effect would a change of government have?

What will successive budgets bring?

2. Economic:

What will happen to exchange rates or interest rates?

What effect will recession or expansion have?

What are the effects of changing levels of unemployment?

How will investment levels change?

3. Cultural and social:

How will population growth change requirements?

What change of life-styles can be expected?

What will be the effects of personal and corporate re-location?

4. Technology:

How will technology change people's expectations?

How will technology influence the transfer of jobs and earnings?

What new products will become available through evolving technology?

5. Institutions:

How will the nature of the traditional institutions alter?

Will the nature of the business and the organizational structure of our customers alter?

Will some of the manufacturing or distributive institutions alter or disappear?

6. Competition:

How will our organization be affected by increased competition?

What conflicts will be created by competition outside our market?

What would be the effect of rapid rises in imports or exports?

Exercise: You may find it helpful to spend a few moments considering what questions your organization, or an organization well known to you, should be asking under each of these headings.

Identifying the competition

To be useful, the examination of the environment has to be objective. For many organizations, it is in the area of competition that objectivity seems most difficult to achieve.

Do you find it easy to assess accurately the competitors of your own business, or the competitors of a firm you know well? If not, what do you think causes the difficulties?

It may be that you either greatly overestimate or severely underestimate the competition you face. Many people do one or other of these things, principally because they look at competition from their own standpoint rather than from that of their customers. This means that they tend to identify competitors on the basis of product processing methods and product features, rather than in terms of product benefits and ways of meeting market needs. With personal computers, for instance, this approach would mean assessing competitors on the basis of the type of microchip circuitry used and the elegance of the software. A much more useful comparison would focus on the ability of the various computers to provide what the personal computer user wants: ease of use, flexibility and the ability to grow with the user.

We are, after all, in competition with whomsoever our customers put us into competition with; whether we think they are logical or right to do so doesn't matter. And, by approaching competition from a customer's perspective, we are automatically focused on product benefits rather than features. This means that we are less likely to overlook competition from firms that sell products which look different from ours, and are made differently, but which provide similar benefits to customers.

Exercise: Take a minute now to reassess the identity of your business competitors from this viewpoint. Have you added some to the list and crossed off others?

The whole picture

When the internal analysis is taken together with the external analysis, the result is an all-round picture of the current situation. This is usually known as a *situation analysis* or *marketing audit*. The process of developing a situation analysis almost inevitably results in the accumulation of a mass of information. This is the raw material for analysing marketing opportunities in order to identify the most promising.

Possibly the most powerful, and certainly the most widely used, technique for structuring the analysis of the information is SWOT. The initials stand for **S**trengths of the organization, **W**eaknesses of the organization, **O**pportunities in the market-place and **T**hreats (especially competitive threats) in the market-place.

SWOT analysis

Figure 8.1 gives a layout and some general guidelines for undertaking a SWOT analysis.

ORGANIZATION **STRENGTHS**	ORGANIZATION **WEAKNESSES**
Only things you are good at that the customer wants go in here. Avoid bland statements like 'professional' or 'experienced' which have little meaning.	All the things you can't do or the competition can do better go in here.
MARKET **OPPORTUNITIES**	MARKET **THREATS**
List here all those parts of the market that you find attractive. Include all the areas where you can predict that change will affect you positively.	A threat to you may not necessarily be a threat to your competitor. Situations in this box will happen whether you stay in business or not.

Figure 8.1.   The SWOT analysis

Strengths and *weaknesses* relate to the findings of the internal analysis. This part of the SWOT analysis involves establishing which facets of an organization constitute its strengths and which its weaknesses – from the point of view of the customer. A strength is something the organization does well which adds to its 'offer' in the eyes of the customer. Conversely, a weakness is something the customer wants which either the organization cannot offer or offers less successfully than the competition.

Exercise: How do the strengths of your competitors compare with your organization's strengths in terms of a 'total offer' to the customer? And what about the weaknesses?

Market *opportunities* relate to findings from the analysis of the external environment. Trends and events are identified which will have the effect of opening up demand for products that meet particular requirements. For instance, the trend among the educated middle-class to adopt 'healthier' eating patterns opens up demand for a whole host of food products, including organic wholemeal bread, skimmed and semi-skimmed milk and snacks made without refined sugar or preservatives.

Market opportunities are, however, just one side of the coin. It is equally important to identify market *threats* – likely trends or events that will reduce demand for certain types of products. Looking again at the above example, the same trend towards more 'natural' eating is a threat to demand for highly processed convenience foods containing chemical additives.

Exercise: What are the main threats in the market likely to face your organization, or an organization well known to you, in the next five years? Why do you see these developments as threats?

It is important to remember that the same piece of information cannot appear in both the positive and negative boxes of a SWOT analysis for an individual firm. Any one attribute cannot be both a strength *and* a weakness, an opportunity *and* a threat. However, the varying *implications* of any one piece of information may be classified into both 'strengths' and 'weaknesses'. Take, for example, the case of a company which has a brand leader among its products. The 'strengths' box may contain:

> a high market share

> a strong market image.

The 'weaknesses' box, on the other hand, may contain:

the company is 'labelled' – that is, so closely identified with one product that development in other markets is difficult.

A similar situation arises when there are alternative scenarios for a market trend; and, depending on which one prevails, the company will face either an opportunity or a threat. The choice of action in this situation lies between:

1. making the assumption that one scenario is more likely than the other and working with this assumption
2. undertaking different SWOT analyses, reflecting the different forecasts.

In fact, the second option is an academic one only; in practice, no organization could proceed on this basis. Out of SWOT emerge the *real* market opportunities – that is to say, the market developments which a firm has the necessary strengths to exploit.

It is important to remember that the attractiveness of a market depends largely on the strengths and weaknesses of the assessor. For this reason, an opportunity for one business may well constitute a threat to another. Similarly, the definition of any factor as a strength or a weakness depends largely on market conditions. The same organizational factor may constitute a strength in one market and a weakness in another.

Checklist

Before embarking on a course of action in the market-place, an organization should:

seek to identify *real* market opportunities: that is, those opportunities which best match the capabilities and circumstances of the firm

in pursuit of these opportunities, carry out an *internal analysis* of its resources and an *external analysis* of its environment carry out a SWOT analysis on the information collected

assess potential market development in the light of the strengths and weaknesses revealed by the analysis.

9 Marketing Research

Clearing the ground

> **Exercise:** What does the term 'market research' suggest to you? And what about 'marketing research'?

On the first, your answers may vary from 'questionnaires' to 'street interviews'. On the second, you may well have drawn a blank: 'marketing research' tends to be a much less visible activity.

In fact, 'market research' is generally used to refer to research into a particular market – its size, structure and the way it is split between competitor companies. 'Marketing research', on the other hand, is a much broader concept, embracing investigations into *all* activities involved in the marketing of goods or services. Such activities could include obtaining information on products, advertising, underlying buying motivations, distribution and sales, as well as the aspects covered by the more narrow term 'market research'.

What's the point of marketing research?

By now it should have become obvious that information is an essential ingredient of sound marketing; information, that is, about the firm itself (both its resources and operations), customers, markets and competitors, as well as the broader environmental issues. But information doesn't just happen; it has to be collected – and this is where marketing research fits in.

The results of marketing research can help management to identify the best market opportunities open to the firm. Use of these results can also, and at the same time, reduce the risks involved in capitalizing on these opportunities. In these ways, good marketing research can directly improve marketing efficiency and effectiveness.

Furthermore, the findings of marketing research are useful as a basis for setting marketing goals and targets for short-, medium- and long-term plans. Because these goals are based on knowledge of existing markets, they tend to be more realistic, and hence more motivating, than objectives plucked from the air.

Marketing research, then, is basically a tool to help management make sensible marketing decisions. In some cases, research may serve to *define a problem*. Let us say, for instance, that sales in our organization have declined. Is the cause product failure, increased competition, a change in consumer taste, or poor promotion? Marketing research can help to provide the answer, and thus enable management to take the appropriate course of corrective action.

In other cases, it may serve to *define alternative courses of action*. Let us say that sales have declined as the result of a competitor's price reduction. What courses of action will cancel out the effect of this reduction? Marketing research may be used to predict the consequences of particular strategies by specifying the relationship between sales and the variables in each decision option. For instance, if the price of a product is lowered by 10 per cent, by how much, if anything, will unit sales increase? Also, how are the firm's competitors likely to respond to such a move?

Research may also serve to *test one or more alternatives in the market-place*. For example, several television commercials may be prepared and shown in different local markets. By measuring the change in sales in each market and adjusting the data for differences in population and income, the most effective commercial can be identified and selected for nationwide viewing.

Another possibility is that research may serve to *test a hypothesis*. For example, management may feel that a new package design will increase sales, then turn to marketing research to determine if this feeling is correct.

In using research to generate information, it is vital to remember that information is an aid to decision-making – not a substitute for it. Information clarifies and rationalizes decision-making by replacing guesswork with facts and enhancing intuition with additional knowledge. Although research seldom automates decision-making, it can organize inquiry and make it more efficient and productive.

Why is it unrealistic to expect research to replace executive judgement? The reason, quite simply, is that marketing managers base their decisions on many more factors than just the information derived from marketing research. They take into consideration a vast array of intellectual and emotional inputs, most of which could not be accounted for in any given research project. Moreover, marketing decision-makers are members of a professional and corporate social system that places many constraints on their decision options.

Types of research

Marketing research can be divided into two broad categories: desk research and field research.

Desk research

Desk research involves the compilation and analysis of information that already exists. However, this information has often been collected for some reason other than the solution of a marketing problem; and the person who initially collected the information may well be external to the organization.

Internal desk research is concerned with an organization's own records; these will usually include invoices, profit and loss accounts, stock control records, delivery notes and salesmen's report cards, as well as previous research reports. From these sources it is possible to build up a picture of such things as:

sales by product group and individual item

sales by customer type

sales by geographic region

customer turnover

number and type of new customers

average credit period

average order size

order cycle time

  drop sizes

  marketing costs – selling, distribution, promotion

  customer opinions

  competitor activity

  trade gossip.

There are also many *external* sources of published information useful to the desk researcher. First of all, there are official government
statistics. Virtually every country has some form of statistical office
which publishes data on all kinds of significant economic and social
factors. Very often such data can be supported and amplified by
reference to the publications of quasi-official bodies, such as trade
and research associations. These usually seek to deal with a specific
area in greater detail than official statistics.

  In addition, much useful information is available from the press,
from trade directories, information services, television companies
and the BBC, market research reports, professional bodies and
banks, as well as – a result of recent developments – on-line data-
bases.

  Many large companies have information centres that either have,
or will obtain, the relevant publications. For firms which do not
have these facilities, the library system provides a good alternative.

Field research

Sometimes the information required will not be available through
desk research; in these circumstances, field research is usually
needed. Even so, desk research will generally provide an essential
background to the fieldwork, highlighting the fundamental problem
and identifying precise information needs.

  Field research involves going out into the market itself – usually
a costly and complicated operation. Indeed, it is precisely because
it is so costly that fieldwork should be used only where desk research
is inadequate. This type of research should not be chosen as a first
option.

  The methods normally used in field research are drawn from the social sciences and use statistical sampling techniques. Three main areas are included in field research:

1. Ad hoc surveys where information is needed for a short-term marketing purpose and hence is obtained on a once-only basis. Observation, self-completed questionnaires, personal and telephone interviewing may be used for this purpose.

2. Continuous research where information is obtained on a continuous basis in order to reveal short-term fluctuations in the market. Continuous research may involve the use of the retail audit system and the consumer panel method.

The *retail audit system* determines the actual sales over a specified time, area and type of outlet. The method used is to make a physical check on retail stock levels and combine these findings with the information obtained from delivery notes and invoices. From this process, actual sales can be calculated.

Since the sample of shops visited is representative of the various types of outlets and areas, much valuable information can be obtained through this method, specifically:

> rate of sales by area and by type of outlet
>
> sales by brand and pack size
>
> retail purchases
>
> percentage distribution.

The method is factual and is generally free from interview bias, but has the limitation that it does not reveal who buys the product or why.

The *consumer panel method* uses a representative sample of consumers. The subjects record their weekly purchases in a diary provided. The diaries are then returned to a processing centre where the information is analysed, in order to reveal changes in consumer purchasing behaviour.

3. Motivational research. In this type of research, concepts from the behavioural sciences are used to try to elicit the true motivations of consumer behaviour. Techniques used include word association, sentence completion, the shopping list, psychodrama and story telling.

How can you choose?

What kind of information comes from these different types of marketing research, and how can you choose which kind of information you need?

All research information can be divided into primary data and secondary data.

Primary data is information which is gathered with a specific marketing purpose in mind and which may not be published or readily available. An example could be information, derived by interview, on buying practices in the chain-hoist market.

Secondary data is information which has been gathered and collated without a specific marketing purpose in mind. Government statistics provide a good example of this. The prime purpose here is to serve the needs of government rather than of business.

Exercise: Take a moment now to glance back at the types of research which have just been described. Jot down which types are likely to yield primary data and which are likely to provide the researcher with secondary data.

You'll probably agree that, on the whole, desk research is likely to come up with secondary data (after all, documents like sales invoices were not drawn up in the first place to shed light on marketing problems); while field research will almost invariably produce primary data.

Both types of data have advantages and disadvantages for the researcher. Secondary data arising from internal research, for example, is likely to be up to date, quantitative (that is, allowing precise measurement) and relevant to the company; *but* it will cover only the firm's part of the market and will not provide information on competitors or on the industry in general. Secondary data arising from external sources may well be out of date and, since it is likely to come from several different sources, may be of variable reliability and classified too broadly to be of immediate practical use.

Primary data, on the other hand, also has a number of limitations. The major criticism of field research is probably that results can be misleading. In fact, this is generally a criticism of the *interpretation* of the data obtained rather than of the techniques themselves. Nevertheless, field research techniques do have their limitations. These include:

> *limitations of accuracy*: statistical error, interview bias, and so forth.

> *limitations of time*: much field research takes a considerable amount of time to set up and carry out. This may render it impractical when marketing decisions have to be taken rapidly.

> *limitations of management*: the organization of field research requires detailed planning and co-ordination. The efforts of different groups of people have to be directed and monitored; and, in some cases, personnel may need to be trained in the appropriate techniques.

Research in context

The appropriate use of research information can enhance the professionalism of a company's marketing function and reduce the intuitive 'hunch' element which all too often can lead the way to expensive marketing mistakes.

As we have seen, research itself cannot make decisions. It merely provides information. Like a signpost, it does not take you to where you want to go, but indicates the direction in which you should travel in order to reach your destination.

If marketing research is to live up to its promise, however, it must occupy a carefully thought-out place in the organization's marketing strategy. It must fit in with the overall context of marketing planning and it must be thoroughly planned, organized and executed. A systematic approach of objective setting, planning, execution and report-back should be taken to each piece of marketing research in the attempt to avoid wasted effort.

How much does research cost?

Research and information are not free. They incur costs in terms of time, effort and money. Before embarking on any research, therefore, the marketer should apply two acid tests to his or her project:

1. Is it likely that the marketing decision would be different if this information were known? If the answer is 'no', it is usually better to save resources for a future situation where the answer is 'yes'.
2. Is the value of the information greater than the cost of obtaining it? If not, second thoughts should be given to undertaking the research.

The financial resources of a company require careful consideration at all times. The number of alternatives in which a company can invest its limited financial resources is so large that research often falls by the wayside in favour of other investments which have a more tangible and quantifiable return.

However, research is not inevitably expensive. Much highly relevant information can be obtained at small cost from company records and from published external sources. The use of desk research, for instance, only requires establishing a definite policy and making a small financial investment. Through its contribution to improved marketing decision-making, well-targeted research can save this investment many times over.

Checklist

Before embarking on a marketing research project, you should:

assess what information you need – and why you need it (what marketing decisions depend on your having it?)

decide what kind of research will give you the information
you require; that is, will desk research or field research
(or both) be most appropriate to your circumstances?

plan in detail how the research will be carried out

ensure that the results of the research will be available in
an accessible and useful form.

10 The 'Right' Market

Concentration of effort and resources

In marketing terms, sales are of two distinct types:

those which are achieved through *reactive* marketing

those achieved through *proactive* marketing.

Exercise: Note down what kind of activity you think might be associated with (a) reactive marketing, and (b) proactive marketing.

Reactive marketing occurs where a company is simply *reacting* to a customer inquiry. Such inquiries can come from all kinds of quarters and can be spread far and wide. A good example of this can be seen in inquiries from overseas. Without too much difficulty, companies can find themselves supplying the odd customer in many different countries throughout the world.

Provided that they are profitable, such sales are very hard to refuse, regardless of where they come from. Indeed, profitable sales of this kind should not normally be refused *unless* they interfere with the company's regular customers or with the plans which the company has made for the future. If either the company's future planning or the quality of service and delivery to its regular or its 'best' customers is adversely affected by casual sales, then management should think again about responding readily to such customers. (Working out just which customers are the 'best' at any given time is a process greatly assisted by careful application of the 80/20 rule discussed in Chapter 6.)

Too many reactive sales are likely to dilute a company's 'proactive' marketing. This kind of marketing involves the activities which a company consciously and purposefully carries out in order to reach the type of customers it most wants. Promotional direct-mail shots or carefully calculated differential price levels might be examples of such activities. Proactive marketing usually requires the commitment of significant marketing resources and investment.

Since no organization, however large, has unlimited resources, individual firms have to accept the fact that they will be unable to do *all* the things they would like to do. This means that they must concentrate their efforts and resources to the best effect. In practical market terms, this can be translated into the general rule that small companies should attempt to tackle fewer market segments than should large companies.

Exercise: Can you think of any other reasons why concentration of effort is usually a sensible approach when an organization is faced with a competitive market-place?

You'll probably have suggested, quite rightly, that a company that does *not* concentrate its efforts – that is, a company that spreads its marketing resources out thinly – will not be in a position to compete effectively in a market-place where competitors have been at pains to give of their marketing best. The company that has failed to con-centrate will find itself with less time to gather information (and make redeemable mistakes), less money for promotion, less selling time, and so on.

Let us take a look now at the main strategies available to organiz-ations for 'targeting' their markets. The first approach – and apolo-gies must be made in advance for continuing the military metaphor – is generally known as the 'blunderbuss' approach. This involves deploying marketing resources and effort across a wide range of targets, in the hope that some of the ammunition will hit the market somewhere, somehow. This approach is not uncommon – but it is certainly wasteful.

The second approach is known as the 'rifle-shot' strategy. Here, the organization will probably have done rather more homework on its market and will be in a position to select and pick off the market segments that look most promising. Clearly, the organization taking this approach will be using its resources in a much more concen-trated. and much less wasteful. way. However, the fact should not be ignored that this second option can be an extremely risky one. Since a great many eggs are put in one basket, the organization is made potentially very vulnerable to adverse trends in the market-place. For example, what happens, in a situation where what had *seemed* to be an unquestionably promising market segment – and one which had consequently attracted considerable marketing resources – suddenly loses its attractiveness on account of some quite unforeseen event or development? The answer, of course, is that the organization with the 'rifle' in its hands would have nothing left to shoot at – and would have wasted all the ammunition which it had gone to such expense to acquire.

Clearly, a balance has to be struck somewhere between these two approaches; just what that balance *is* (in terms of what marketing activity where) will depend on the circumstances of the individual organization. However, it should be noted that, on the whole, more marketing failures result from excessively broad targeting than from excessively narrow targeting. In other words, in marketing, 'rifles' tend to be more effective than 'blunderbusses'.

The firm which has decided to concentrate its efforts and special-ize in certain market segments can expect to reap other benefits as well. These include:

> the opportunity to develop a deep understanding of its market, along with the requirements, motivations and buying patterns of its customers

> the ability to use this understanding to make more accur-ate forecasts of market trends. This, in turn, will put the firm in a better position to develop successful new prod-ucts and to plan future directions of development

> the opportunity to achieve a high market share and all the benefits this brings. High market share – that is, a high proportion of sales in a given market – is a relative term. In fragmented markets, 10 per cent may be enough to be significant; in monopolistic markets, nothing less than 50 per cent will do. It is important to remember too that the market at issue may not be the total, national market. It

máy be a particular market sector or segment; the only relevant market-share figure is that which relates to a market which the firm actually serves.

Selecting the 'right' market

The individual firm will almost always be concerned with selecting the most appropriate *market segments* rather than the markets themselves. On the whole, 'markets' are too large and too broad in scope to represent a meaningful unit for marketing purposes.

But how does the firm work out which market segments it should concentrate on? The answer lies in bringing together the results of the market segmentation exercises (discussed in Chapter 5) and the SWOT analysis (discussed in Chapter 8). Additional commercial appraisal can then be applied to the findings; and a sound marketing decision can finally be taken.

In Chapter 14, on the 'right' product, we shall explore in greater detail how the firm's offering can be successfully matched with the market segments selected.

What makes a market the 'right' market?

So, given limited resources and the need to concentrate its marketing efforts, what sort of factors should the organization be looking at in order to choose the best market options available?

Aim for 'distinctive competence' in the market-place. As we saw in Chapter 8, the starting point for any organization is the selection of markets or market segments which best match the capabilities and resources of the firm. This usually means aiming for market segments where the firm has some 'distinctive competence' (that is, some positive attribute, quality or strength which singles a firm out from its competitors). If the firm lacks a distinctive competence, then it should aim to move the business into an area where it *can* display this attribute.

Select on grounds of market knowledge.   The firm is most likely to succeed in those market segments which it knows well. Such knowledge should cover identity of the customers, the nature of their needs, the trends in the market and the factors that influence customer choice.

Be aware of internal considerations.   Does the firm have the ability to meet the new market opportunity? In other words, are company policy and resources such that the firm can effectively provide the 'total offer' required by the market?

Choose the market segments which match the firm's plans for the future.   The 'right' market segments will be compatible with the firm's desired direction of growth and development. Let us suppose, for example, that the firm intends to go 'up market' in its market presence. In this case, the choice between market segments should fall on those which contain customers with a high disposable income, etc.

Concentrate on market segments with size and growth potential.   The best market prospects are those segments enjoying growth and expected to reach a significant size.

Avoid segments where the competition is cut-throat.   Most companies entering markets effectively 'carved up' by strong competitors will run into serious trouble sooner rather than later. Even where there is obvious disenchantment on the part of customers, entry into a market of this kind is very risky. Of course, there are the exceptions. Some firms have entered highly competitive markets and won. But the fact that these firms can be identified individually illustrates just how rare this phenomenon is.

Assess the barriers to entry.   Barriers to entry into a market include such factors as the expense of entry and the degree of technical competence required. If the firm is already in a market characterized by such barriers (such as the market for quality sound systems), then the barriers work in its favour and it should concentrate its efforts on that market. If the organization has not yet entered the market, it should assess whether the high investment costs involved can be recouped sufficiently quickly to make entry worth while.

Check that the segment offers a sufficient level of profitability.   Is there any indication that the market segment offers profitable sales? Some segments just do not offer commercial firms the level of profitability they require.

Maintaining the 'right' market

In thinking about the 'right' market, organizations forget at their peril the fact that markets are in a constant state of change. The marketing strategy that is 'right' on entry into a market may not be appropriate after a period of time. Companies must constantly adjust their marketing stance in order to meet and anticipate the changes occurring in a market. To continue the military metaphor, they must treat the market as a constantly moving target where the sight and positioning of their firearm must be adjusted continuously if the target is to be hit. Sometimes it is easy to see the right target; it is often quite another matter to score a hit.

Checklist

In approaching the selection of the 'right' market, organizations should:

> analyse how they can concentrate their marketing efforts and resources to the best effect

> weigh up in terms of their own business the pros and cons of the 'rifle-shot' versus the 'blunderbuss' approach to targeting markets

> assess the benefits which a carefully planned 'concentration' could bring to their business

> study the findings of their market segmentation exercises, along with the results of their SWOT analysis

apply commercial appraisal to the market choice which this study suggests

assess their choice of market segments in terms of the following factors:

'distinctive competence'

market knowledge

internal considerations

segments compatible with the firm's future plans

segments with growth and size potential

segments without cut-throat competition

no overwhelming barriers to entry

sufficient level of profitability.

3 The Technology of Marketing

11 The Product as a Market Offering

What is a product?

Well, what *is* a product? Or, indeed, a service? (For the purposes of discussion, the word 'product' from now on will be used to cover both goods and services.)

Exercise: Jot down your answer to the question, 'What is a product?'.

Now compare your answer with the following definitions given by some of the different people intimately concerned with making and selling a company's products:

to the R & D department, a product means some technical innovation

to the production manager, it means making a material object to an agreed specification within cost and time constraints

to the sales manager, it means the end result of the manufacturing process which must be sold at a given price in the most efficient way

to the distribution manager, it means an object which must be packaged and transported in various quantities to various destinations, within constraints of size, weight, perishability, and so on.

to the customer, a product is what he or she buys.

Which definition is most similar to your own initial answer to the question, 'What is a product?' What do you think this tells you about your attitude to marketing?

The differences between the various definitions of a product may appear to be trivial; from the marketing standpoint, however, they are extremely significant. If the marketing concept is accepted, by far the most important point of view is that of the customer. This means that successful marketing depends on the organization looking at its products in terms of what they give to the customer. (You may have noted, quite rightly, that in some cases the distributors, or intermediaries, are in fact the immediate customers for the product; shouldn't their perception of the product therefore be equally important? Indeed, it should. In such cases, the company must strive to offer a product attractive to both the immediate customer, the distributor, and the end customer, the consumer.)

As we have already seen in Part One, what the customer buys is much broader than the material object (or basic service) that the company has produced. In the case of a physical object, for example, the customer may acquire packaging, before- and after-sales service (including spare parts and maintenance), guarantee, credit facilities, company reputation and experience, as well as the all-important, but much less tangible, *benefits* that ownership is expected to bring.

From the customer's point of view, the product is not just a combination of parts but is a *consequence* of the combination of these parts. Thus, the customer intending to purchase a car will not be interested in the car's engine as such (that is, in the different mechanical parts that are combined to make up an engine) but in the *performance* that the engine can provide. The material object is only a means to an end and not an end in itself. As Theodore Levitt puts it: 'People don't buy things – goods or services. They buy the expectations of benefits: not cosmetics but the allurements they create for their users; not quarter-inch drills but quarter-inch holes; not common stocks but capital gains; not numerically controlled milling machines, but trouble-free and accurately smooth finished parts; not

Dream Whip but sophisticated convenience.' The significance of a product does not come from what it consists of, its features and its attributes. Instead, it comes from the wants and needs people are trying to fulfil with the benefits derived from the product features. To the customer, a product is a solution to a problem.

Exercise: Think about the main product offered by your own organization or by an organization well known to you. Why do customers buy this? *What* in fact are they buying? What benefits do they expect to gain as a result of buying this product?

The danger of 'product myopia'

It is not unusual for firms to concentrate myopically on the products they supply rather than on the market needs those products meet. This short-sighted orientation is reflected in the way businesses are described by those within them, and by the sales literature they produce. All too often, the customer is left to translate what the various features of a product (such as its format, method of operation, material construction and arrangement of component parts) mean in terms of benefits provided.

What happens if a firm, or even a whole industry, fails to look at products from the customers' point of view? Basically, it gets left behind. This is because, although the needs of customers change imperceptibly slowly, the ways in which these needs may be met, and the degree to which needs are met, change rapidly.

Look at the railways, now a declining industry. For many years, railway managers focused their attention on the trains and the track rather than on the customer. Customers were expected to seek out the railway, rather than vice versa. Meanwhile the road transport industry displayed considerable sensitivity to customers' varied needs, and developed products to meet those needs. The result was that while the railway industry declined, the road industry prospered at its expense. Had the railway's managers seen themselves as being in passenger or freight transportation (that is, become customer- or market-orientated) instead of in railways (that is, remaining product-orientated), the industry might be in a better position today.

The same can be said of the entertainment film industry. There is no sign of any slackening in the demand for personal entertainment. But there are great changes in the types of personal entertainment being sought – and the trend is away from watching films in cinemas. Despite this, few production companies in the film industry made serious early moves into areas of growth, such as television, mainly because they continued to see their business as one of making films. However, more recently they have been quicker to work with, rather than against, the boom in home videos.

Any organization must, therefore, view its products from two main standpoints. In the first place, it will take a *corporate standpoint*, assessing the product in terms of its fit within the business. For example:

> Does the firm have the appropriate engineering capability and skills to manufacture the product?
>
> Does the firm have sufficient resources to distribute and sell the product in the most appropriate way?
>
> Can the firm cope with any marketing research needed?
>
> Can the firm develop appropriate advertising and promotion strategies?
>
> Can the firm afford the necessary investment in the product?

But, in the second – and equally important – place, the company must also view the product from the *customer's standpoint*. This means asking questions of the following type:

> What satisfaction does the product provide?
>
> Is it good value?
>
> How does it perform in use?
>
> Is it conveniently available?
>
> What basic customer need does the product meet?

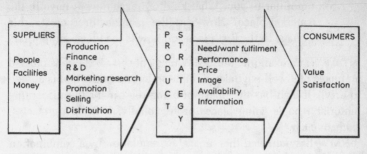

Figure 11.1.   Product strategy

How can the right customers find out about it?

How can they be persuaded to buy it?

Does the price seem right?

Figure 11.1 illustrates the different factors to be considered by the firm in developing its product policies and strategies.

The product – one member of a team

A product does not stand alone. It is, as we have seen, only one part of the 'total offer' made to customers. Furthermore, its very identity is affected by the context in which it exists in this total offer. The promotional message that accompanies it; its availability; its price – all these work together in the eyes of the customer to create an overall 'image' of the product. This image reflects the 'perceived value' of the product – its quality, purpose, usefulness, status, uniqueness, and so on.

It sometimes appears that businesses forget the basic principle that the product *cannot* be viewed in isolation from the other components of the marketing mix. This basic mistake nearly always stems from failing to look at the product from the point of view of the customer. 'Getting the product right' is important – but it is not enough. Nothing less than getting the 'total offer' right is enough.

Exercise: Think for a moment about a high-quality consumer item familiar to you. What kind of image does it have in the market-place? How did the manufacturer create this image in the first place and how is the image supported?

Take, as an example, the BMW range of cars. BMW has created an image of a well-engineered, high-performance car that is superb to drive. It also has the image of being *the* car for the discerning motorist who is going places professionally. It is an up-market, exclusive car.

BMW has achieved this 'image' or reputation by a combination of strategies. First, it produces cars to a high specification and continually makes changes, or improvements, to those specifications. (And, in its early days, BMW took care to educate potential customers to understand, appreciate and want the technical features in a car that BMW was offering.) Secondly, the firm's promotion always overtly emphasizes the technical superiority of the vehicle – but it does it in a way which reinforces status and exclusivity. Thirdly, as far as price is concerned, BMWs are not cheap! Price is rarely mentioned, but the impression is always strongly conveyed that BMWs are expensive, on the lines of 'If you have to ask the price, you can't afford it'. Finally, place. The number of distributors is limited, and these distributors are charged with reinforcing the quality image. Furthermore, BMW actively seeks to limit the number of cars it sells in order to remain exclusive and desirable.

So, the image of BMWs has not been achieved by the product, the car, alone. Rather it has been achieved by the careful blending of all the elements of the marketing mix into a 'total offer'.

How not to be 'Brand X'

The image created by BMW is different from the image created by other manufacturers for their cars – and deliberately so. Why do organizations want their products to be seen as different from other products? And how is this achieved?

The reason is straightforward: to gain a competitive advantage. Indeed the aim is not just to create something that customers see as different, but to create something they see as 'better'. This is because in most markets there are several products vying for sales – and the first step in winning the battle is for a product to be noticed as offering something different.

Of course, as the BMW example shows, it is not the product alone which is differentiated, but the total offer. It is the total offer which firms try to shape into 'Unique Selling Propositions', or USPs.

Look at consumer goods such as coffee, soup, dried herbs, fire-lighters, washing powder, toothpaste and engine oil. In each case the generic product is much of a muchness, yet the individual brands are highly differentiated. The Brand X of the television commercial is really very similar to the named brand. But no one wants to be stuck with selling such a boring, undistinctive, anonymous product. To distinguish products, manufacturers have tinkered with product formulations to make them look, smell or taste slightly different from competing goods. However, branding, packaging, advertising and pricing in fact play a more important role in their differentiation in the market-place.

Exercise: Think for a moment about two providers of the same service – say, banking, insurance, dry-cleaning or hair-dressing. What methods does each business use to distinguish its particular service?

The product mix

Of course, most businesses do not sell just one product; they sell several. For many businesses, in fact, it is the very assortment of their product mix which is central to providing customer satisfaction. Retailing, where the *selection* of products made available for sale is all-important, is a good example of this.

Exercise: You may well have come across the terms 'product mix', 'product line', 'product range' and 'product varieties'. What do you think each one means?

Check your answers against these. The 'product mix' is all the different products sold by an organization. A 'product line' is a set of closely related products. These normally fall within the same product class. In the case of Procter & Gamble, for instance, soaps, washing powders, shampoos and toothpastes are just some of the product lines within the overall product mix.

An individual product within a product line is often referred to as a 'product variety'. 'Head and Shoulders' shampoo for normal/dry hair in a 300ml bottle size, for example, is one product variety within Procter & Gamble's shampoo product line.

Finally, the 'product range' of a business is the sum total of all its product lines.

BREADTH ⟶ OF PRODUCT RANGE

	Basic box file £2.50	Basic lever-arch file £1.60	Basic expanding file £4.50	⟶etc.
DEPTH ↓ OF PRODUCT LINE	De luxe box file £3	Executive lever-arch file £2.20	Expanding file PVC-covered £6.60	
	Box file double strength £5.25		Reinforced expanding file with extra pockets £12.50	
	Box file double strength with manilla index £5.75			
	↓ etc.			

Figure 11.2.   The product mix: part of the product mix of a commercial stationery firm

Figure 11.2 illustrates the way all these terms are connected.

Needless to say, the broader and deeper the product mix, the more complex is its management. When varieties and lines are added, but seldom deleted, it is very easy for a product mix to become unwieldy and virtually impossible to manage effectively. The tools and concepts introduced in the chapters which follow provide a framework for managing the product element of marketing, and for keeping it under some sort of control.

Checklist

In making an assessment of the product part of its marketing mix, the organization should:

identify the customer benefits associated with the product

analyse how well the product fits in with the rest of the business

analyse how well the product fits into the 'total offer' available to customers

take into account the need for creating, where applicable, a 'product line'

while recognizing the need for variety, remember to keep the product range down to a manageable level.

12 Product Tools and Concepts

Thinking strategically

So far, we have looked at products principally from the all-important viewpoint of the customer. Products cannot be brought to the market at all, however, unless a whole host of organizational factors are correctly matched with customer perceptions.

Exercise: Some of these factors were mentioned briefly in the last chapter. Can you recall what they were?

Bringing together an organization's resources to get a suitable product on to the supermarket shelf or into the mail order brochure requires the setting and resolving of a vast and at times bewildering array of management questions.

The problems are complicated enough even for a small firm with only one product. In modern business organizations, it is common for any one company to market dozens, or even hundreds, of products simultaneously. Experience has taught marketers that it pays, strategically, not to keep all your corporate eggs in one product basket. Thus, using the jargon, organizations are said to keep a 'portfolio', or range, of products.

Just to complicate matters yet further, nothing ever stands still. We live in a fast-changing business world. Changes in technology and taste, the emergence of new competitors, the shifting patterns of financial constraints and opportunities, all conspire to give marketers plenty to think about, including many strategic reasons for changing the product portfolio – for adding promising new ideas and dropping yesterday's winners.

The juggling of so many factors at once could – and frequently does! – end up in chaos and confused thinking. Help is at hand, however. The emerging science of marketing has come up with some powerful conceptual tools, by means of which the product strategy of an organization can be made a great deal clearer. These tools provide, for example, means by which the balance of the product portfolio can be related simultaneously to the organization's cash-flow needs, its production capacity and distribution and sales resources, as well as the current or potential performance of any particular product in the market.

Let us unveil two of the most important conceptual tools in question. They are:

    (a) the concept of the 'product life-cycle' and
    (b) the Boston Matrix.

The product life-cycle

       This concept is based on the observation that products, like their customers, have a life-cycle during which they are born, grow to maturity, enjoy their prime of life, grow old and eventually die – unless, as is often the case, they are unsentimentally eliminated when they cease to be useful – the products, that is, not the customers!

Products can be, and nearly always are, eventually displaced. It may be that a vastly superior product comes on to the market, like stainless-steel razor blades; or a more convenient way of doing something is developed, such as the automatic camera. Certain kinds of need may even disappear altogether: not many people still wear long-john underwear, for instance, now that many houses are well heated and insulated; and the demand for grate-blacking is no longer what it was!

The *length* of the life-cycle depends on the nature of the product. Fashion products – pop records, for example – generally have very short life-cycles, whereas electric light bulbs have been regular purchases ever since the demise of the candle and the Dickensian gas lamp. All products, however, have a recognizable cycle of rise and decline which marketers find it useful to monitor closely, especially for the immense range of products subject to technical development and changes in customer taste.

Five principal phases of the cycle are of particular significance:

1. Introduction or launch: Sometimes a new product is first brought to market before demand for it has been proven and often before it has been totally debugged technically. Typically, at this stage, sales are low. Awareness and public acceptance are minimal. One marketing implication of this phase is that advertising should aim to make the likeliest potential customers *aware* that the product is available.

2. Growth: This is the 'take-off' stage when demand for the product accelerates. As this stage becomes established, potential competitors may enter the market. Product and brand differentiation may begin to develop. The company's marketing problem shifts away from creating awareness and towards getting the customer to prefer its own brand.

3. Maturity: Sales growth continues, but at a declining rate, and indeed sales are nearing a peak. Saturation of the market may be drawing near; that is, there are few potential customers remaining who are unaware of the product or who have not got around to purchasing. Competitive products may be too strong to allow further market share expansion. The marketing thrust at this stage is to maintain sales at current levels.

4. Saturation: Sales reach a plateau, consisting basically of customers buying replacements for their first or subsequent purchases, when the earlier purchase wore out, or for whatever reason. Price competition now becomes intense. Competitive attempts to achieve and hold brand preference now involve making finer and finer differentiations in the product, in customer services and in promotional practices and claims made for the product.

5. Decline: Sales begin to diminish as the product is edged out by better products or substitutes. Some companies may decide to 'milk' the product dry; others will withdraw it from sale. By this time, new products should have been phased in, so that initiative is retained in the market.

Exercise: Our comments on the above five stages all emphasize features of the customer-orientated, demand side of the marketing operation. How might these stages be of significance to the production side as well? How can reading the runes of the cycle help production planning? (Clues are to be found in Figure 12.1.) We have already described the sales curve in the notes above. But what do you make of the pattern of cash generation? And of profit?

You'll see that both are actually negative in the early stages of the product's life. For a while, the product actually makes a loss, and an even longer period elapses before sales generate sufficient

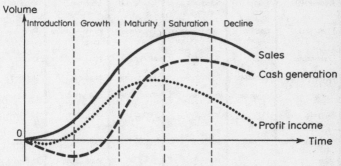

Figure 12.1. The stages of the product life-cycle

revenue so that it becomes possible to pay off the debts used to finance the introduction of the product or to contribute surplus cash to finance investment elsewhere in the company.

Just as the development of a child into an economically independent adult requires an expensive investment of time, education and training, so a product too must be supported in its early stages. And since this support needs planning, it makes financial sense, from the corporate point of view, to have a family of products that are spaced out at different stages of their life-cycle. It helps enormously in the management of production capacity, too: if you *know* well in advance that certain of your products are nearing the end of their useful life, you can plan their withdrawal from the market in co-ordination with the launch of others, using, in many cases, the same production facilities.

Thus we begin to see the wide implications of the product life-cycle as a marketing tool. There are many more such implications which an introductory text like this cannot go into. But just casting an eye over Figure 12.2 will give you some idea of the many strategic factors that marketers can monitor and plan, using the cycle concept.

	Introduction	Growth	Maturity	Saturation	Decline
Growth rate	Good	Rapid	Slowing	Plateaued	Negative
Sales	Small	Growing	Peak levels	Falling	Disappearing
Profits	Break-even	Peak levels	Level	Falling	Disappearing
Cash flow	Negative	Break-even	Good	Good	Falling
Predictability	Hard to define	Some certainty	Well defined	Uncertain life-expectancy	Known and limited
Product line	Specific/ narrow	Rapid expansion	Differentiation	No development	Rationalize
Competitors	Few	Growing	Many rivals	No new entrants	One or two left
Customers	Innovative	Early majority	Late majority	Laggards	Mass exit
Strategy	Expansion	Penetration	Consolidation	Defend share	Productivity
Marketing expenditures	High	Very high	Reducing	Discounting	Minimal
Communications	Awareness	Product	Loyalty	Selective	Residual
Price	High	High	Lower	Price-cutting	Rising
Ease of entry	Easy/ high risk	Safe	Hard	Unwise	Foolish
Technology	Important role	2nd and 3rd Generation	Emphasis on process technology	Material substitution	Stable

Figure 12.2.   Characteristics of the stages in the life-cycle

Before we leave the product life-cycle, we must touch on one fairly sophisticated difference of opinion among marketing analysts as to the meaning of the word 'product' when we speak of a product life-cycle. Different texts make different assumptions, and this could cause confusion unless you are aware of the issues.

Individual products, such as the renowned Model-T Ford or the Morris Minor, quite plainly had a complete life-cycle of their own. But this cycle, the life of a *particular* brand or model, while being the most obvious area for applying the concept, may not be the most *relevant* product life-cycle for the most profound aspects of strategic analysis.

The brand/model life-cycle may be very important in relation to issues of a company's own cash-flow/production situation. But when that same company looks outwards, as it must, to the market at large, it often makes more sense to consider *industry* sales and profits within a particular product–market, not those of a particular brand. Individual products or brands may be introduced or withdrawn during any stage of the product life-cycle. Further, their sales and profits may fluctuate up and down throughout the life-cycle – sometimes moving in the opposite direction to industry sales and profits. Market leaders may enjoy high profits during the market maturity stage – even though industry profits are declining. Weaker products, on the other hand, may not earn any profit during any stage of the product life-cycle.

What a company *can* fruitfully monitor as regards its own brands/-models is their performance in relation to industry product life-cycles (or the 'product–market life-cycle', as it is sometimes known) in order to gain a clearer picture of the situation at any given time.

The Boston Matrix

We now turn to the second of our conceptual tools, the product portfolio matrix, or the Boston Matrix. This bears a relation to the stages of the product life-cycle, in that it also classifies products by their stage of development – although in this case using rather more colourful terminology. In broad terms, the product designation of the Boston Matrix equates to the product life-cycle stages as shown in Figure 12.3.

The matrix itself, developed by the Boston Consulting Group in the USA, is based on the perceived importance of maintaining a high share in growth markets. It thus aims to relate the growth situation of a product – and we are now talking about a company's *specific* brands or models – to the competitive situation, in terms of

Product life-cycle	Boston Matrix
Introduction	Question marks
Growth	Stars
Maturity / Saturation	Cash cows
Decline	Dogs

Figure 12.3.   The connection between the product life-cycle and the Boston Matrix

the market share held by the product. Figure 12.4 shows the matrix in its conceptual form. As we shall see, organizations can fill in the matrix with their own product portfolio and see at a glance many vital ingredients of their strategic product marketing position.

Before turning to how the matrix is used, let us look more closely at the beasts that comprise this singular menagerie.

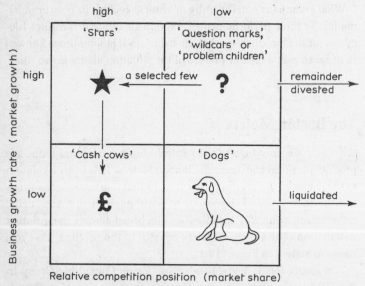

Figure 12.4.   The Boston Matrix

Question marks: Question marks are high-growth, low-share products. Because of their low share, it is assumed that they require a lot of cash to maintain or increase their share. These products are called 'question marks', 'wild cats' or 'problem children' because it is not clear what to do with them. Management has to decide whether it wants to spend more money, if they have the potential to become market leaders, or, if not, to phase them down or out.

Stars: Stars are high-growth, high-share products. It is usually assumed that these are, or will be, profitable products, although cash is needed to finance their rapid growth. Generally, it is assumed that financing stars is desirable because eventually, managed properly, they will turn into cash cows – which will become major cash suppliers for other products.

Cash cows: Cash cows are low-growth, high-share products, generating cash to develop other products. The strategy is to maintain their position as economically as possible.

Dogs: Low-growth, low-share. These are the old favourites. They may have sentimental value, especially those on which the company's prosperity was originally founded, but they may by now have come to represent a drain on resources of time and money that would be more profitably deployed elsewhere. These are the prime candidates for deletion.

The above very general description is applicable to all sorts of products. Individual organizations, however, are interested in their own particular product portfolio, and how well balanced it is. They can find this out by plotting the position of all their own products on the matrix.

Exercise: Take a few moments now to consider how the products of your own organization, or of an organization well known to you, might slot into the categories of the Boston Matrix. What overall picture does this exercise give you of your company's product portfolio?

The most obvious information to be obtained from such an exercise is the answer to the question: 'How well balanced is the portfolio?' An unbalanced product mix can lead to cash-flow problems in a company. Too many products in the lower left segment (low-growth, high market share) will result in an excess of cash but nothing to invest in. Conversely, a company with too many high-growth products will face periods of severe cash shortage. The advantages of such a chart are many. It is possible to tell at a glance a company's profitability, debt capacity, growth potential, dividend potential and competitive strength.

Exercise: What do you notice about these kinds of information?

Well, the issue of profitability goes to the heart of any company's concerns. So do debt capacity, dividend potential and cash-flow, but these are all essentially *financial* matters, not ones which we have seen so far as coming within the domain of the four 'P's of marketing. One important function of the Boston Matrix then, and to a lesser extent of the product life-cycle, is to enable market conditions, including the customer preferences central to market-ing, to be related back to the kind of products that are generated, and to the financial considerations that make production possible. Here we see the matching process, between the customers' needs and the organization's resources, at a most integrated level.

Having looked at these major conceptual tools, in the next chapter we turn to a more detailed view of product policy and some key stages, including the introduction of new products and the phasing out of old ones.

Checklist

In developing a sound approach to the planning of its product–market strategy, the organization should:

think in terms of a balanced product portfolio

consider use of the product life-cycle concept to assess and monitor the progress of its products in the marketplace

consider use of the Boston Matrix to assess the overall balance of its product portfolio.

13 The Evolving Product Range

Where do products come from?

Given the complexity of the questions surrounding product selection by the company, it is clear that no product should appear overnight in the market-place. In order to come up with a product that jointly meets company and market needs, management must put considerable work into the preparatory stages of product development.

New product planning takes time as well as effort. The process may involve market investigation, technical design, tooling and reorganization of production and, possibly, the setting up of a new distribution system.

There are many sources of new product ideas, some of which are:

> Research and Development
>
> company personnel
>
> market research
>
> technological and scientific discoveries
>
> competitors
>
> other countries
>
> unused patents.

The problem is not usually one of obtaining ideas but of eliminating those ideas which may not lead to satisfactory profits, and of selecting those which will. This is usually done through a screening process which considers the ideas in the light of what is known about the market and the company's resources. After this initial screening, a programme should be drawn up to ensure that the investigation will proceed within agreed limits of cost and time.

The aim of screening is to minimize financial outlay and personnel time, and the process continues throughout product development. After the initial ideas have been identified and scheduled for investigation, a second screening will investigate the possibilities in greater detail, perhaps under the following broad headings:

1. the market
2. company resources
3. competition.

The market

The market for new products will depend upon the degree of innovation; that is, just how 'new' the new products are. New products can be grouped into the following categories:

> completely new products. The market for these is totally unknown

> improvements to existing products. Here a market already exists and can therefore provide some indication of the likely acceptance of the improved product

> products which are already available in the market, but which have not previously been offered by the company

> existing products, available in other world markets but which have not previously been on sale in the company's own local geographic market – for instance, they may have been available previously in the US but not in the UK.

In practice, most new products are developed through product line extensions and product improvements. The commercial stationery manufacturer whose box files were featured in Figure 11.2, for example, could add a 'new product' to his box-file line simply by offering another type of box file with a tab fitted, to make it easy to pull the file off the shelf. The launch of such a product, requiring relatively little special investment, is unlikely to be accompanied by elaborate market testing programmes.

On the other hand, some types of product improvement demand investment of resources on the scale of entirely new products. Where this is the case, management may well need to ensure a carefully planned introduction to the market-place.

Regardless of whether the product is new or just 'new looking', the following factors should be taken into consideration:

(a) The potential demand for the product: This will involve quantifying the number of likely customers, both in the first stages and in future time-periods. The effect on demand of advertising and other forms of promotion must also be assessed.

(b) The likely life-cycle for the product: This will depend on many factors – for example, the rate of technological change, and the ease with which competitors can develop and initiate production of a similar product.

(c) The volume and price: Some indication is needed of the volume and price which must be achieved to generate sufficient profits over an acceptable pay-back period. Pricing in particular is a delicate decision area and involves deep consideration of the company's entire market strategy and competitive position.

(d) To what extent the product can be further developed: Some thought should be given to the possibility of further development or modification to cater for additional markets and/or market segments. For example, with modification, an industrial product may have potential in the domestic market at some future date.

Company resources

(a) Finance: Is sufficient finance available, and how will the expenditure affect the cash-flow position?

(b) Production: Thought should be given to the capacity of the existing plant and the opportunities for expanding the capacity. The availability of land, for example, along with local and national government restrictions and incentives are obvious points for consideration. The manufacture of a new product may involve additional personnel, some of whom may require training.

(c) Marketing: Will the existing distribution channels be suitable for the new product, or will a new system need to be set up? The sales force will have to be trained in the new product, but how much training will be required? Can the product be patented? Can it be sold under the company's brand name without adverse effects on the existing product range? How well are the marketing needs of the new product likely to fit in with existing marketing expertise and practice?

Competition

How many competitors will we have for the new product?

How do their resources compare with ours?

What is the likely lead time before competitors can develop a new product which will affect the profitability of ours?

Are competitors developing a new product which may make ours obsolete?

These are just a few of the questions that need to be addressed at this stage of screening.

The screening process, then, is highly complex. However, only if a new product idea can pass successfully through this kind of examination should it be allowed to progress through the next stages of new product development. These can be summarized as:

development – the turning of the ideas into prototypes.

testing – the conduct of commercial experiments to validate earlier findings.

commercialization – an all-out launch of the product, backed by the company's full reputation and resources.

As you might expect, this extensive screening process, followed by test marketing, results in many would-be products falling by the wayside. This is illustrated in Figure 13.1.

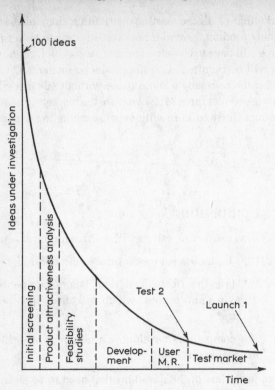

Figure 13.1.   New product development failure rate

Product development

Having survived its initial screenings for viability, the promising new product idea can now undergo a detailed business analysis. This consists of a close study of investment requirements, revenue and expenditure projections and financial analysis as regards return on investment, pay-back period and cash-flow.

Now, at last, the product itself can begin to take shape, in the form of a few prototypes. These enable the engineering and manufacturing of the product to be considered in detail and also make it possible to produce sample products for market testing.

This development stage is sometimes highly sophisticated, taking years of research. Intensive research is not confined to high-tech products like aero engines or compact discs. Often the lengthy time-scale involved reflects the to-and-fro relationship between production research on the one hand and market research on the other. It took Procter & Gamble, for instance, over ten years' work and $80 million to develop a new kind of potato crisp in the USA!

In some cases, screening only starts once the prototype has been developed. In firms where engineering traditionally takes precedence over marketing, for example, the initial screening of product ideas may be omitted.

Test marketing

The Procter & Gamble crisp is flat, and can be packed and stored more like biscuits than ordinary crisps, with consequent economy of space and a long shelf-life. This involved technical product development which itself took a lot of time to get right.

Also time-consuming was the process of refining the product concept. This had to be carried out after different versions of the product were tested on various selected individuals and groups of potential customers. Eventually a few of the most successful variants were tried on large numbers of Procter & Gamble employees.

Such *placement tests*, as they are known, are a standard procedure for many new products.

So are *market tests*, where for the first time the product is actually sold to customers through the usual channels – though with sales probably restricted to a single geographical test area. At this stage, different varieties of the product can be tested at different retail outlets, or in different areas. Variations in the marketing mix can also be explored for the first time, such as alternative brands, prices or advertising copy.

Sometimes test marketing is not practical. Fashion goods, for example, could hardly survive a ten-year development with full test marketing and still expect to be in fashion! Durable goods too, with high fixed production costs and long production lead times, may have to go directly to market. There is all the more need, in these cases, for the early stages of product selection to be carried out carefully.

Commercialization

By the time the company's resources and reputation are fully committed to a major new product launch, the complete marketing mix – the entire strategic plan – must be fully in place; the product must have the backing and enthusiasm of top management; and tactics for expanding sales in line with company resources and production capabilities must be clearly laid down.

Product elimination – why get rid of products?

The opposite of new product development is product elimination. It is every bit as vital to rid the product mix of products which are 'past it' as it is to add rising stars. However, this is a less glamorous activity and so tends to receive less attention.

In the past, some firms have let their product range grow and grow. They have steadily added new products but failed to delete any old ones. The trouble with this approach is that a very wide and deep product range is impossible both to manage and to sell effectively. Furthermore, obsolete products tend to take up an inordinate amount of management time and resources. Despite this, many firms have shown a marked disinclination to eliminate products from their range – to the extent sometimes of even failing to notice the harmful effects caused by carrying obsolete products. It remains the case, however, that delays in this area invariably prove costly.

Exercise: Can you suggest some reasons for a firm being disinclined to delete old products? You may find it helpful to think, for example, about the way in which many marketing departments are organized.

Now compare your answers with the following suggestions:
   1. Many marketing departments contain 'product managers' or 'product group managers'. These are the people most likely to know which products are candidates for deletion. However, they are *also* the people with the greatest interest in keeping 'their' products alive.

2. A firm may well have a sentimental attachment to a product – especially if the company's prosperity was founded on it.

Given that a systematic programme for product deletion is essential, how does the firm decide when to delete individual products? When a product is technically obsolete or just plain old-fashioned, and when sales volumes and market share are stagnant or declining, the decision is a clear-cut one. But what about a situation in which a product is making a profit, and looks like doing so for some time ahead? Why are these products sometimes also deleted? What sense can there be in throwing away profit?

A firm may delete a profit-making product when it can be seen to be entering the decline phase of its life-cycle. Its best days are known to be over; keeping the product going is diverting the firm's production capacity, sales staff time, financial resources, management time and attention from other, potentially more profitable products. So, in fact, the firm is *not* throwing away profit when it eliminates a product in decline. On the contrary, it is throwing away a *larger* profit – or incurring an *opportunity cost*, as the economists say – if it decides to retain the product.

There are circumstances, however, in which a firm may make a deliberate decision to keep a product that is not making any contribution at all. The reasons for this decision may include the following:

the product is an integral part of the product mix

the product keeps competitors out of the market

the product is demanded by key distributors

the product contributes to the overall corporate image.

One reason, then, for deciding to delete an apparently profitable product is the judgement that the product is entering the decline phase of its life-cycle. A further reason for a decision of this kind is that the product fails to fit in with the company's present positioning or declared direction for strategic development.

Let us look at the food industry, for example. Many food manufacturers are now producing more natural products without chemical additives or preservatives, in line with the growing interest in healthy diet. At the same time, some of these manufacturers are also deleting their preservative-laden lines (though these are still profitable) because of the perceived adverse effect these lines are having on their overall image.

Elimination, in other words, can be used to reinforce corporate image.

It is worth noting that while whole systems for new product development have been devised, product deletion methods are very variable and *ad hoc*. This offers some indication that so far there has been far too little interest in deletion methods and strategies.

Strategies for elimination

1. *Individual product*

The product in question may have failed to establish itself or it may have been superseded in the market-place. In this case, the strategy is usually simply to drop the product. The Sinclair C5 electric vehicle is an example of a stand-alone product which failed to establish itself in the market and has subsequently been dropped.

2. *Line simplification*

Line simplification describes a situation where a product line is trimmed to manageable size by pruning the number and variety of products or services being offered. A confectionery firm, for example, which might have a hundred or more brands, flavours and packagings, is likely to prune its lines regularly and routinely, cutting out those items with the lowest profit, sales volume and growth potential.

3. *Line divestment*

Sometimes it makes strategic sense to drop an entire product line, perhaps by selling off the business division that handles it. Divesting the firm of assets in this way became an accepted option with the advent of strategic planning in the 1960s: this strategy came to be seen as a means of generating faster growth.

A divestment strategy does not always involve ridding the company of an *unprofitable* division or plant. Many organizations have found themselves in the position where they support the divestment of a *profitable* product line. The main reason for this is likely to be the desire to release assets for use in other parts of the business which are more in line with the strategic focus of intended future development. For example, STC is a communications company that, anticipating the closer relationship between communications and computers, bought ICL and established a corporate mission of computer-based communications. Associated with this development has been extensive divestment by STC of non-computer-linked business. The divestment has been made not because of any unsatisfactory financial performance in these areas, but because they no longer fit in with the new direction of the company's growth.

Exercise: Does that sound familiar? Compare it with what was said earlier in the chapter about *opportunity cost* and image reinforcement.

Reviving a product's fortunes

The birth *and the death* of a product can be seen as important points in the product life-cycle at which marketing decisions must be made. Ultimately, though, the metaphor breaks down. A product is not a human being. Certainly it can be killed off prematurely; but it may be possible – if the option looks a sensible one – to invest heavily in its revival, to reincarnate it, if you will, setting it off on a whole new life-cycle.

Exercise: Think, for example, about *The Times* newspaper, owned by News International, an organization which also controls the profitable, but scarcely prestigious, *Sun* and *News of the World*. Why might News International have decided to retain, and further invest in, a loss-making product like *The Times*?

At the top of your list will probably be the comment that *The Times* makes a positive contribution to News International's corporate image.

Exercise: What can be done to reincarnate an ailing product? Perhaps the most obvious thing is to improve the product, to bring it up to date, or make whatever other changes are considered necessary. What other options does your marketing knowledge suggest to you? You should be able to think of at least three other items, based on the four 'P's.

Checklist

In working towards a balanced product range, organizations should pay particular attention to:

new product planning. This will probably involve:

a rough screening of new ideas for likely winners

a more detailed screening for (a) acceptability to customers, (b) compatability with company resources, (c) robustness in the face of competition

a programme of product development

test marketing

commercialization

product elimination. This will probably involve the adoption of one or more of the following strategies:

individual product deletion

line simplification

line divestment

14 The 'Right' Product

Meeting what needs?

The glib answer to the question 'What is the right product?' is: that product which best meets both the needs of the market and the requirements of the organization. The answer may be glib, but the essence of a fuller and more helpful answer nevertheless lies within it. As will be seen, the expanded answer, in this chapter, looks more closely at both 'the needs of the market' and 'the requirements of the organization'.

The strategies available

The 'right' product can only be chosen in the context of the strategy employed by the organization for exploiting market opportunities. Organizations have basically a choice of four product–market strategies:

1. *market penetration* – more sales of existing products into existing market segments
2. *market development* – selling existing products into new market segments
3. *product development* – selling new products into existing market segments
4. *diversification* – new products into new market segments.

Which strategy? – The question of risk

With these four strategies open to a business, how might a choice be made between them? The rest of this chapter explores the means open to an organization for making such a choice, in the light of its own particular product possibilities.

136   *The Technology of Marketing*

A very general point to be made, irrespective of particular businesses and their markets, is that opportunities should be developed with a minimum of risk. Sometimes the potential for a high pay-off may make it worth while to go for a high-risk development, but the organization should at the very least be aware of what types of product developments carry which levels of risk.

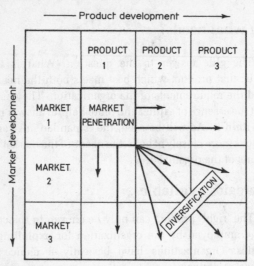

Figure 14.1.   Product–market strategies

Look at Figure 14.1. The illustration shows, in positions 1, 2 and 3 on each axis, the most straightforward, low-risk possibilities for extending the business.

If a firm has a strong product range, it will be asking, 'Who else can we sell our products to?', and will be seeking to sell into further markets 1, 2, 3, etc. (vertical axis). If customer interest and loyalty are evident in existing markets, the firm may instead be asking 'What else can we sell them?', and will try to develop more products 1, 2, 3, etc. (horizontal axis).

These are the most obvious areas in which to develop new opportunities. Ideas of this kind should emerge from the audit process described in the next section of this chapter.

If opportunities here genuinely don't exist or have been exhausted, then the next strategy is to concentrate on another source of strength: the technological and managerial strongpoints of the organization: so-called 'process strengths'. What new customers would buy which new products arising from our technological or organizational strengths?

This approach implies a policy of *diversification*, of reaching out into the relatively uncharted waters shown by the arrows in the diagram. In general, this policy is a risky one; but use of one of the organization's process strengths can provide some security. However, it should be noted that it is sometimes difficult to be objective about exactly what a genuine strength is in the process area.

Diversification without using any of these three strengths – product, customer or process – is the equivalent of starting a new business. This is the most exciting area of all, where most companies do their development and meet their Waterloo.

We might note also that, at the safer end, it is safest of all to go for market penetration, but this alone cannot contrive to support sustained growth. Whether a business goes for product development or market development should depend essentially on its area of strength. As we have already observed, though, many firms exhibit a product-orientated bias which leads them to think only about selling their existing, over-favoured products into new markets, when the scope for this may be limited. So mistaken *product*-orientation can lead to the wrong road (in this case) of *market* development.

Products and SWOT analysis

The idea of SWOT analysis was introduced in Chapter 8 with reference to identifying opportunities in the market.

Exercise: Remind yourself what the letters S, W, O and T stand for. When considering all the factors that go to arriving at the 'right' product, how might this type of analysis be helpful?

Think about it, using what you know about your own organization, or a company of which you have some knowledge. How might the company:

build on its recognized **S**trengths and use the process of systematic 'auditing' to tease out hidden sources of strength?

remedy **W**eaknesses?

build on market **O**pportunities?

avoid, or counter, market **T**hreats?

As you will probably have concluded, the 'right' product can be labelled as such only in the context of a firm's situation in its marketing environment at a given moment in time. This position will be revealed by the situation analysis and summarizing SWOT.

Strategic planning grid

A technique, or tool, for identifying which products might best match which market needs, to the mutual satisfaction of the

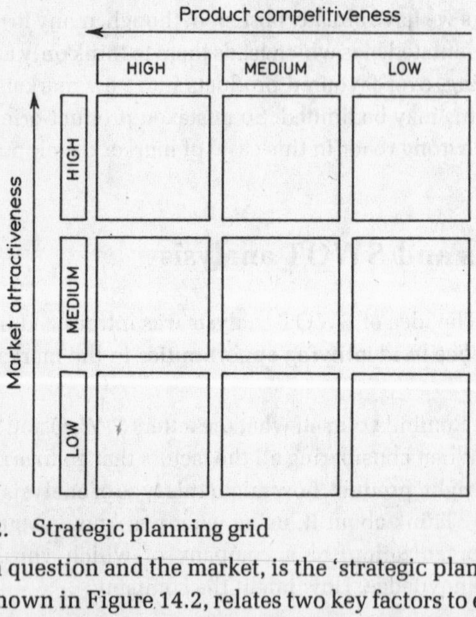

Figure 14.2.   Strategic planning grid

business in question and the market, is the 'strategic planning grid'. The grid, shown in Figure 14.2, relates two key factors to each other. These are *market attractiveness*, which answers the question, 'Do we like the look of the market?' and *product competitiveness*, or 'How well do we think we can compete?'

Indicators of market attractiveness include:

> How big is the market?
>
> What is its growth rate?
>
> What is the cost of entry?
>
> What is the concentration of competitors?
>
> How high is product loyalty?
>
> How accessible is it?
>
> How profitable are its occupants?
>
> What technical expertise is required?
>
> How compatible is it with existing operations?

Indicators of product competitiveness:

> Do we have a USP (Unique Selling Proposition)?
>
> Can we achieve high quality?
>
> Can we develop or source the product?
>
> Can we make it?
>
> Can we market and sell it?
>
> Do we have distribution potential?
>
> How can we offer after-sales service?
>
> Is there sufficient value added?
>
> How investment-intensive is it?
>
> Do we have adequate manpower/finance?
>
> How compatible is it with existing operations?

The response to each of these screening questions is capable of being ranked on a high/medium/low basis. Thus, the most attractive product possibilities and most attractive market possibilities come together on the top left corner of the grid, giving a clear indicator of the appropriate product–market strategy.

The right portfolio

The right product strategy requires the right product mix, as well as products which are individually useful.

Exercise: Think back to what we learned in Chapter 12 about using the concept of the product life-cycle and the Boston Matrix as aids to generating a balanced portfolio of products. You will probably remember that generating a balanced portfolio involves both a sound new product development programme and a thorough product elimination system.

What we have considered so far in this chapter is the larger strategic perspective: how, by looking at the fundamental matching process between the organization's resources and the customer's needs, it is possible to arrive at the right product and the right balance of products.

Theoretically, this is all that is required. Before going on, however, it is worth looking more closely at some of the more important – or less obviously important – points that contribute to the attractiveness ratings of the strategic planning grid.

1.   Is the new product compatible with the existing business and can it co-exist happily with current products? Most companies have more than one product and it helps if the result is a mesh, not a mess. A new product does not have to 'fit into' existing lines as neatly as a cog in a machine. It may be an entirely new departure, a diversification, but it must be compatible – a valuable add-on component to the machine rather than a spanner in the works.

2.   The product should have a strong USP. That is, the product should be clearly distinguished or differentiated from others avail-

able to the customer. It is the extent to which a firm's 'total offer' is seen as different (in a positive way) that determines the answer to the question, 'Why buy from them?'

3. Ideally, the product should have the potential to be the best and therefore the leading product in its target market segments. In large companies this may well mean a high share of a large target market segment or even a national market. For small businesses, it may mean tight, concentrated targeting and identifying market niches in which it is possible to be dominant. A milk roundsman might, for instance, aim to concentrate his efforts on a specific district rather than a widely spread area; that is, he may decide that it is better to deliver to every household in one road than to a few in one road and a few in another several miles away. The small company can fare better if it is a big fish in a small pond, whereas the big company may want, or even need, to be a big fish in a big pond.

Exercise: There are many ways of measuring market share. Take a moment to think of a few possibilities, and jot them down. Remember that it is important to assess tomorrow's *potential* market as well as today's actual one.

There is general agreement, though, that, however measured, high market share is an advantage. The benefits involved are as follows:

the products begin to sell themselves on reputation

greater volumes of the same product lead to economies of scale in all functions, bulk purchase and delivery, and a faster ascent of the experience curve

a buffer against the onslaught of competition

influence over market pricing

higher margins that can be returned to the customer in the form of innovative new products, better service

more efficient promotional spending to attract new customers

> a reputation that aids entry into new markets, provided there is some linkage between products.

High market share is a relative term. In fragmented markets, 10 per cent may be sufficient to be a significant force; if there are few competitors, nothing less than 50 per cent will do.

Finally, did you manage to think of any of these measures of market share? Share of: market turnover, customers, wholesalers/retailers, volume consumed, activities performed, market profits.

4. *High market growth.* The ideal product will serve a high growth market because here the potential for the product, and hence the business, is greatest. High growth markets also tend to be less directly competitive – especially in terms of price.

5. *Relatively low investment* needs are a favourable factor. Better returns tend to be achieved by such products.

Those who are first to introduce a product to a market have an edge in the early stages over competitors entering the market. As markets change at an even faster rate, however, this competitive edge does not always last long enough to generate returns at a sufficient level to offset the cost of expensive new product investment. Such investment might accompany the development of any new product – a new chocolate bar, for example, a meat pie or a consultancy service.

In short

What is the main significance, then, of the different approaches and techniques discussed in this chapter? Quite simply, they are aids to determining which products to market. Unless the organization identifies the product–market strategy and the product mix most appropriate to its circumstances, then it is unlikely to be able to offer the market the 'right' individual products.

Checklist

In assessing the 'right' products for their markets, organizations should bear the following factors in mind:

> a number of product–market strategies are available:
> > market penetration
> > market development
> > product development
> > diversification
>
> low-risk options are the safest
>
> SWOT analysis clarifies the possibilities
>
> strategic planning grid enables favourable market factors to be matched with favourable product factors
>
> product life-cycle and Boston Matrix can be studied to generate a well-balanced product portfolio
>
> indicators of product–market attractiveness include:
> > new product compatible with existing ones
> > strong USP
> > high potential share of market segment
> > high market growth
> > low investment needs.

15 *Distribution as a Market Offering*

Placing 'place'

'Place' is perhaps the most intangible of the four 'P's. After all, despite the complexities which we have found to surround it, the 'product' can be pinned down and described without too much difficulty; the importance of the 'price' component can readily be grasped; and as for 'promotion' – well, we can all visualize sales interviews, television commercials, brochures, and so on.

But what about 'place'? What kind of thinking and activity is carried out by an organization's distribution function – and why is it so important? Is 'place' *really* on an equal footing with the three other components of the marketing mix?

Exercise: You may care to note down here some of the activities which you would expect to be associated with a firm's distribution function. From the customer's point of view, why are these activities important?

Let us now take a look at some examples which illustrate the very real importance of the 'place' element of the mix.

Imagine that you are out one Saturday afternoon; you feel peckish and decide you fancy something to eat, like a bag of crisps, say. Most people expect something like crisps to be sold almost everywhere – from newsagents and supermarkets to kiosks and pubs. So, if you go into the first appropriate retail outlet and see the crisps you want, you'll probably buy them almost without thinking. But what if the crisps you want are not available – what do you do then? Go else-where? For a product like crisps this is a most unlikely course of action, unless you have an extremely strong craving for them. What is more likely is that you either abandon the whole idea or buy a substitute – a packet of salted peanuts perhaps. Whichever decision you make, it amounts to the same thing: a lost sale for crisps for one reason and one reason only: they were not available in the right place at the right time.

Take another example. A few years ago a leading manufacturer of electrical appliances launched a particularly compact travel iron. The product idea was 'right', the launch timing and promotion were 'right' and the price was 'right'. But there was still a problem: it was almost impossible to buy one because the shops just didn't have them to sell. Something had gone awry with the distribution planning to such an extent that most shops ended up receiving their launch stocks weeks late. Soon afterwards another manufacturer came out with an almost identical product. It is *this* version that is now stocked by most of the high street multiples and which most people buy. The high street retailers stock it because deliveries have always been reliable, and the customers buy it because it is the one most readily available. Through not having 'place' properly sorted out, the original manufacturer has lost both the marketing initiative and a lot of money.

Finally, consider the challenge facing suppliers of a commodity like industrial salt. Industrial salt from any supplier is essentially the same, and prices tend to be on a par. So why do manufacturers favour some suppliers over others? Mostly, it is because of delivery. The salt supplier with a reputation for reliable deliveries will nearly always score over the supplier who delivers either early or late, but rarely as arranged. Indeed, in many industrial-commodity-type markets, it is the 'customer service' provided by the distribution or 'place' element of marketing that distinguishes one firm's 'total offer' from another in the eyes of the customer.

So, basically, distribution is all about getting products to where they are wanted, when they are wanted. For crisps, this means having them always readily available in as many outlets as possible, so that consumers can pick them up to buy with the minimum of trouble and fuss. For carpets and furniture, it may mean having samples on display in appropriate outlets for ordering, with delivery to the home several days (or weeks!) later. And for an industrial-component manufacturer, it may mean having a system of telephone ordering with regular and reliable weekly deliveries.

Working towards customer service

As the above examples show, there are two sides to distribution or 'place'. First, there is making products available for purchase; this is the *trading* side of distribution. Secondly, there is making products available for use by the purchaser, which is the *physical distribution* side of place. In some cases, both aspects of distribution follow the same route or channel; but this does not always happen. Agents sell products without physically handling them, for example, and third-party distributors handle products that they never own or sell. Managing and co-ordinating the two sides of distribution to ensure that the customer receives the service required is looked at more closely in the next chapter.

You may remember reading in Chapter 11 that, on the whole, customers are not interested in the nature of the combination of different parts which go to make up the product; instead, they are interested in the *consequence* of the combining of the parts. That is, they are interested not in the car engine as such but in the resulting *performance* of the car – in other words, they are interested in the *benefits* of the engine, not in its features. The same is true with regard to distribution or place. Customers are not really interested in how products are made available to them. Rather, they are interested in the level of customer service they receive – that is, in the benefits rather than the features of place.

The term 'customer service' has now been mentioned several times; but what is it exactly? Quite simply, it is the service given to a customer once a decision to buy has been made. It should include such things as the ease of placing orders, order–delivery cycle times, delivery dates (and their reliability), outlet location and parking facilities, after-sales service, the way customer inquiries are handled, and even the manner adopted by delivery drivers, shop staff and receptionists towards customers.

Retailers sometimes use the term in a different context: in-store 'customer service' may refer to refund or cheque cashing facilities or to gift voucher buying services. Physical distribution and logistics specialists, on the other hand, will use the term 'customer service' to mean either the number of orders fulfilled from stock or the number of days in which a given percentage of orders can be met in full.

Both of these definitions of customer service are specialist ones and narrower in scope than the broad 'marketing' definition described above.

Exercise: Now, choose a product that you know well. What customer service is provided by the various suppliers? How much does the level of service vary? What are the main areas for improvement? In carrying out this exercise, you may notice, first, that there seems to be a market norm for customer service and, secondly, that individual firms have not made the most of distinguishing themselves from others by using this area as a positive marketing tool.

'Place' in different contexts

The challenges posed by distribution vary according to the type of business involved.

Most retailers, for example, find that the location of the shop is the most important aspect of 'place' for them. Indeed, it has been said that the three most important factors in the success of a shop are location; location; and location.

To a manufacturer of consumer goods, 'place' means the distribution of products to customers by means of retail outlets. In this instance the distribution task therefore involves fulfilling the expectations of both intermediaries and final customers. The difficulties inherent in this task are exacerbated for the manufacturer by the need to rely on intermediaries to present, sell, deliver and support the products in a satisfactory manner.

The core elements of 'place', however, are of concern to all types of business. These comprise decisions on:

location of premises

trading channels, that is, buying and selling up to the point where the product is available for the final customer to buy

physical distribution/logistics, that is, getting the actual item to the customer.

Channel relationships

When intermediaries are used in getting the product to the customer, the success of the distribution effort depends on the combined forces of a number of different firms. This means that the manufacturer has no direct 'chain of command', so to speak.

In most areas of marketing, authority and control are likely to be clearly defined and located; and the most common type of co-ordination needed is liaison and agreement between different departments within the one organization. With distribution, however, success depends on obtaining inter-organizational co-ordination. An important facet of distribution therefore consists of managing relations between the different firms involved (or, in marketing terminology, the 'channel members').

The complex negotiations needed in this area raise many questions of power, control, leadership and co-operation. And, as new institutions and trading patterns develop, so balances of power can be seen to shift within the channel. For example, manufacturers traditionally held the balance of power; they used to be able to select their distribution rates and distribution channel members. However, in many areas today (notably in the grocery industry) it is the large distributors – especially the large retail multiples – who have the upper hand and who in effect choose their suppliers.

A further change has also taken place. Traditionally, manufacturers supplied wholesalers who supplied retailers; and all of these channel members operated independent businesses. Now, increasingly, retailers are buying suppliers and manufacturers are buying outlets; furthermore, there are more and more firm contractual arrangements between suppliers and retailers. Franchise groups (like Wimpy and Avis) and symbol groups (like Spar and Mace) provide examples of this trend. In franchising, for instance, outlets are contracted to an organization which not only supplies products but also dictates trading policy.

Co-ordination with other marketing functions

The distribution function depends on the other marketing and business functions, just as they in turn depend on it. As we have seen, failure in any of the main marketing areas will inevitably lead to breakdown across the marketing board. The interface between distribution and certain other main functions is particularly important for marketing success. Such interfaces include:

Distribution/products: Co-ordination is essential if (a) the right stock quantities of the right products are to be achieved and maintained at appropriate times, and (b) the right types of product are to reach the right types of outlet.

Distribution/promotion: The success of any promotional campaign depends on the success of this interface. The distribution function has responsibility for ensuring that adequate stocks will meet increased customer demand following promotional activity. Distribution must also ensure that the place from which the product is sold and the way it is sold are consistent with the promotional message.

Distribution/packaging: Packaging must meet two distinct needs. It must help 'sell' the product in an appropriate way. It must also physically protect the product and allow for easy handling, both by intermediaries and by final customers.

Distribution/pricing: The level of customer service adds value and hence needs to be taken into account when prices are being set. Cash-and-Carries, for example, were able to supply goods at a cheaper price because they provided a lower level of service. As part of a new trading pattern, customers had to visit central premises, select the items they wanted themselves, pay immediately and arrange their own transport of the goods back to their shop. The traditional delivered trade, on the other hand, takes orders over the phone, compiles the orders, delivers them and then sends in an invoice – thus effectively giving customers thirty days' credit.

Distribution/marketing dynamics: In all its interactions, the distribution function must be lively, active and dynamic. Lethargy in this area can easily lead to an overall staleness in the company's marketing effort.

Some trouble-spots

In many organizations, the distribution effort is weighted towards controlling the costs of the physical logistical operation. This is understandable enough since considerable costs are indeed involved here, and the operation itself (involving haulage and so on) is often very visible to management.

However, there is a danger in this emphasis of paying insufficient attention to the distribution function's primary purpose: that of meeting and satisfying customer needs. Considered as a market offering, distribution must mean giving customer service a pre-eminent position.

Checklist

In assessing its distribution as part of the 'total offer' available to the customer, the organization should:

identify what benefits target customers are seeking in terms of availability, convenience, and so on

distinguish between the trading side of its distribution function and the physical distribution side

define what 'customer service' means in its business

have a clear idea of the relationships possible and desirable among the different channel members involved

ensure that the efforts of the distribution function dovetail smoothly with the activity of the rest of the business.

16 Distribution Tools and Concepts

The two sides of 'place'

Exercise: The last chapter introduced you to *two* basic aspects of distribution or 'place'. Check that you remember what the two sides of distribution are, and jot down one example of each to make sure you understand the distinction.

Both sides of distribution are concerned with matching up customer and product in the right place. But the *trading* side of distribution means providing the customer with a *purchasing opportunity* in the right place. Trading is concerned with buying/selling transactions. Generally, money or a cheque changes hands or a credit card entry is made.

Often, when you make a trading transaction, a product does change hands also. When you go to your corner shop to buy milk, you expect to hand over your cash and walk away with a carton of milk in exchange. In this case, the *physical distribution* of the actual product to you, the customer, happens at the same time as the trading transaction.

But remember that this is not always the case. The way that *physical* distribution of products is organized can be separate from the way that *buying* the product is organized. For example, a major Sunday newspaper may carry an advertisement offering its readers the chance to buy, say, a sofa bed, at a special offer price. You, the reader, fill in your credit card number on the newspaper's order coupon and post it off to an address with the newspaper's name on it. Usually, the advertisement tells you that you may expect the item to be delivered to you within, say, twenty-eight days. Having made your *trading* transaction, you, the newspaper reader, then simply sit back and wait for the product to be *physically* delivered to you.

If the product does not arrive within the stated time, though, you may begin to look into the physical distribution side. Perhaps you ring a special 'inquiries' number and ask for an explanation. You might find, say, that the beds are made at a factory in Germany and that delivery is late because of a factory fire . . . or that the road haulage company bringing the products across the North Sea is facing a strike affecting the ferry service it uses. In other words, the *physical* distribution of your sofa bed has nothing to do with the newspaper which sells it to you. If you try ringing the editor to make a complaint, you will not get very far!

When you are thinking about the organization of distribution, it pays to think about *trading* and *physical distribution* separately. This chapter therefore looks first at trading tools and concepts and, secondly, at physical distribution tools and concepts.

The most important key elements to keep in mind are:

(a) trading
    The 'trading channel':
        intermediaries
        channel power
        channel structure
        channel integration
(b) physical distribution:
    the *total distribution* concept
(c) putting the two sides together:
    customer service.

The trading channel

Exercise: In the last chapter, you came across the 'trading channel' as the series of buying/selling links before final purchase takes place. But why is there a need for a series of buy/sell links? In other words, why are *intermediaries* used at all in trading transactions?

Intermediaries

There are various reasons why manufacturers use intermediaries in distributing their products to final customers, and the reasons depend on the type of product. But one common reason concerns the *costs* of making each transaction. The cost saving likely to result from using intermediaries can be shown by a simple example of trading channel geometry.

Suppose first of all that there are three manufacturers of a product, who all want to distribute their product direct to three major customers. Each manufacturer needs to establish a trading link – or

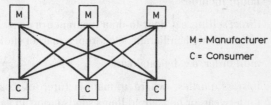

M = Manufacturer
C = Consumer

Figure 16.1.   Distribution contact configuration – I

'contact line' – with each customer, and so *nine* contact links are needed in all. (Figure 16.1.) But now suppose a firm enters the picture as a trading intermediary, offering to buy from all the manufacturers and sell to all the customers. How many 'contact lines' are needed now? (Figure 16.2.)

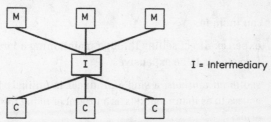

I = Intermediary

Figure 16.2.   Distribution contact configuration – II

If each contact line costs something to maintain, then using an intermediary, which reduces the total number of contact lines needed (from nine to six, in our example), will reduce trading costs overall. It is not possible to cut costs indefinitely in this way, but cost saving is a powerful motive for using intermediaries. To make the benefits of using intermediaries even clearer, let us think for a moment about the alternative – direct selling.

Direct selling

Exercise: Can you think of examples where manufacturers do use direct selling methods without using intermediaries? Make a list of three or four examples.

Examples could include:

> *direct selling*, e.g. door-to-door insurance or encyclopedia sales; selling handicrafts, etc., from a market stall

> *mail order*, e.g. by catalogue

> *hostess parties*, where a manufacturer of cosmetics, underwear, or household items sends along an agent

> *automated vending*, e.g. hot drinks, sweets and cigarettes

> *home shopping* by computer.

Exercise: What do you think are the problems or limitations of using direct selling methods in each of your examples?

Problems can include:

> *expense:* direct selling through maintaining a large sales force tends to be expensive

> *scattered markets:* a single producer is unlikely to have access to as many markets as a producer using intermediaries

> *specialization:* expertise in trading gained by intermediaries enables the service to be offered more cheaply and effectively in many cases

> *bulk-breaking:* a typical manufacturer will produce few product-lines, but in large quantities. A typical consumer will want a wide choice of product-lines, in small quanti-

ties. An intermediary can offer this choice to the customer
by acting for several manufacturers. One manufacturer
alone cannot

suitability: some products are more suitable for direct selling than others; for example, expensive items will not be
secure in a vending machine; clothes sold through catalogues must be fairly standardized.

These problems and limitations of direct selling methods also prompt the use of intermediaries.

Channel power

Many manufacturers do use one or more intermediaries to make up
a 'trading channel' from manufacturer to customer. But the manufacturer then faces a problem of power in the trading channel. Manufacturers frequently complain both about the lack of control they can
exercise over their intermediaries and about their intermediaries'
performance. So who does wield the power in a trading channel?

Who has channel power?

As a generalization it is true to say that in many cases manufacturers'
channel power is now being challenged by the power of large
retailers, especially the large multiple outlets. These days, the large
multiples may even develop new product specifications themselves.
They are certainly in a position to make decisions – for example, on
product-lines carried and on display and shelf space – that affect
consumers' purchasing decisions and are increasingly important to
manufacturers producing for mass markets.

Another source of large retailers' power is the unprecedented
amount of sales information assembled when using Electronic Point-
of-Sales equipment. For example, if you walk into one well-known
late-night grocery's retail outlet to buy a previously forgotten tin of
cat food, by the time you walk out, the sales staff will have recorded
your sex and approximate age, as well as your purchase and its
timing. They will be able to assemble much better sales data than
the manufacturer of pet foods has direct access to.

The recent tendency for large retailers to gain power in the trading channel at the expense of manufacturers is particularly clear in the grocery trade, where well over 60 per cent of groceries are distributed through a trading channel using a grocery multiple store. But the example of groceries also illustrates a useful general point. In grocery trading channels, the typical food manufacturer and the typical grocery multiple are both large firms. It is hard to imagine one wielding absolute power over the other. What we are talking about in trading channels is in fact a *balance of power* between channel members.

How is channel power used?

To see how a balance of power in a trading channel can be maintained, we need to define the concept of power we are using in this context. What is the basis of channel power – and how is channel power exercised?

Exercise: When you think of the word 'power', your first thought is probably connected with *coercion*, making someone do what you want by threat or punishment. Stop for a moment and consider whether coercion is the most likely form of power to be exercised in a trading channel.

Seems unlikely? Then jot down three or four sources of power other than the use of threat or punishment. On what *other* basis can decisions and behaviour be influenced or controlled?

Your list might include:

offering some kind of *reward*

appealing to a legitimate *right* or a *norm*

claiming greater knowledge or *expertise*

and your list may include other bases of power, too. Look at your list and decide whether these forms of power fit the case of trading channel power better than straightforward coercion does. Probably a combination of power sources is in operation. That the *balance* of power in a trading channel may mean coercion is not possible. Even where coercion is possible, it is usually a disruptive, and therefore an expensive, way of exercising power and solving conflicts. When we talk of channel power, we usually mean a more routine and less confrontational way of *influencing* the *behaviour* of other channel members. Influencing the behaviour and decisions of others is what channel power is all about. Often it is only a *potential* ability to influence other channel members; power may exist in a trading relationship without necessarily being exercised all the time.

Exercise: Now glance back at the list of power sources you have just made. Imagine a trading channel in, say, grocery distribution, with just two channel members: a food manufacturer and a supermarket chain. What kinds of examples could each type of power involve?

Rewards could be, say, higher profit margins, extra promotion allowances, or managerial assistance, from the supplier; or, from the supermarket, increased turnover. Rewards will often be the converse of *coercion*, which might take the form of refusing shelf space to a manufacturer, or refusing to stock one product-line exclusively; or a manufacturer refusing to supply popular brands.

Rights may take the form of a contract or else of a norm – say, on turnover. A sweet manufacturer may only agree to supply a retail outlet if it will take three cases of a product-line per week, if that is the norm for turnover.

Expertise might involve either market research data held by the manufacturer or sales data held by the supermarket chain.

What is channel power used for?

Power in a trading channel mostly comes into play when there is a *conflict* or potential conflict of interests between channel members.

Conflicts of interest often arise when *changes* are made to distribution channels. For example, supermarkets have moved into the toiletries area, creating a stimulus for new channels to proliferate in addition to the old channels using retail chemists. Or again, a manufacturer might start to use its own sales force and cease to

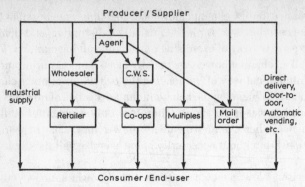

Figure 16.3.   Trading channels

employ agents. This could apply in services, too; British Rail, say, has a choice between selling rail services through travel agents and through its own travel centres.

Power in a trading channel is needed to manage such conflicts and changes and, in general, to encourage channel members to co-operate. Ideally, trading channel members will work as a team. To bring that teamwork about may need leadership from one of the channel members; and the exercise of power is one of the elements making such team leadership possible.

Channel structure

So far, we have looked at a simple trading channel with one manu-facturer and one large multiple retailer in it. But trading channel structures can be more complicated than this. Often, a trading chan-nel is not planned; most channels just evolve. Probably this is because they involve entering into relationships with other firms over which direct power and authority cannot easily be exercised. This makes it easier just to slot into established procedures and practices.

Channel structures for consumer products are rather different from those for industrial products. Figure 16.3 illustrates the range of channels typically found.

Exercise: Look at Figure 16.3. Which do you think is the most commonly used type of channel for
(a) consumer products?
(b) industrial products?

If anything, the 'traditional' trading channel for consumer goods is from producer to wholesaler, then to retailer, then consumer. However, many large retailers now buy direct from the manufacturer. Large retailers include the multiples and the symbol groups, such as V.G. and Spar, as well as the Co-operative shops.

For industrial products, direct channels from producer to industrial user account for the greatest volume (at least, in pounds). For both types of goods and services, however, a variety of channels exists, both direct and those involving agents, wholesalers/industrial distributors and retailers.

Two contradictory forces operate on the decision as to what type of channel structure is best. On the one hand, the benefits from using intermediaries, and from specialization among channel members, push the decision towards a longer and more complex channel. On the other hand, the problems of co-ordination, power and conflict management push towards a more integrated channel, seen as a *system* rather than a chain of loosely linked channel members.

Over the last twenty to thirty years, more integrated systems have been developed, and an increasing proportion of goods and services are distributed through integrated channels.

Channel integration

Two kinds of integration are involved in this process, and both kinds are usually present in today's integrated marketing channels. Horizontal integration occurs when two or more independent units at the same level in the distribution chain combine — two retailers, say. Vertical integration implies combining two or more successive stages of distribution: either manufacturers try to integrate the system 'downwards' to secure distribution of their product line, or else retailers try to integrate 'upwards' to secure supplies, for example of popular branded products.

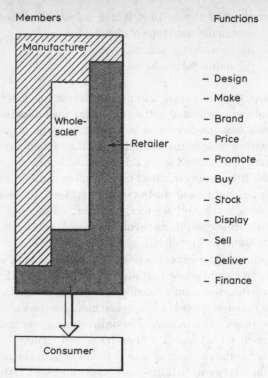

Figure 16.4.   A vertical marketing system

Today's integrated channels are known as *vertical marketing systems* (see Figure 16.4); in these systems the whole range of decisions – from designing and making the product, to pricing, promoting, stocking, displaying, selling, delivering and financing it – are considered as a whole, instead of separating decisions out among the manufacturing, wholesaling and retailing stages, as used to be the case in conventional trading channels.

Integration may be maintained by

> *ownership*, where all stages of production and distribution are combined under single ownership
>
> *contract*, where production and distribution stages are

separately owned, but contractual agreements are made between the parties

power, for instance where a manufacturer can insist on integrated distribution of a popular brand.

Physical distribution

So far we have emphasized that distribution is much wider than physical distribution alone. But physical distribution or *logistics* involves the physical movement of all materials, parts and goods from raw materials to the delivery of the finished product to the consumer or user. This means that physical distribution has two very important contributions to make. First, it contributes to cost cutting. Secondly, it contributes to sales by providing the delivery service customers want.

Cutting costs

The contribution which logistics can make to cutting costs derives from the high proportion of costs – about a fifth of sales revenue, in manufacturing – which is taken up by the physical movement of materials, parts and goods. Improved methods to reduce the necessary level of inventories, to assemble orders automatically, or to make warehousing more efficient, such as one-storey warehouse layout, are all contributions to cost cutting from the physical distribution side. A useful concept for use in maximizing cost cutting is the concept of the *total distribution system*.

Total distribution system

The 'total distribution' approach to logistics or physical distribution management is an approach that requires an overview of all physical movement and handling in the company and one that requires co-ordination of all physical movements throughout production, from materials management to order processing, transportation, warehousing, materials handling, inventory control, packing and customer service. The aim of co-ordinating all aspects of physical

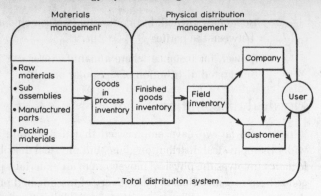

Figure 16.5.   The total distribution concept

distribution in a company through a total distribution system approach is to maximize efficiency and cost cutting (see Figure 16.5).

Exercise: Think for a moment about this approach to physical distribution. What *alternative* approach to organization of the physical side of distribution can you suggest?

The alternative is in fact the traditional approach to the flow of materials, parts and goods, in which its organization is split up between marketing, production, distribution, purchasing, and so on. In the traditional approach, each functional area is responsible for organizing those physical distribution activities falling within its own orbit. No one has responsibility for organizing physical distribution as a whole, and each function may well be oblivious of what the other functions are doing. So, although each function will try to minimize costs for its own *part* of the physical distribution flow, it could well turn out that costs are not minimized in physical distribution *as a whole*. This is one disadvantage of the traditional approach.

Exercise: Can you think of a disadvantage of the newer total distribution approach?

One disadvantage is that, with the focus on saving costs *overall*, trade-offs are necessary. This means that each function may have to accept what it perceives to be shortcomings in the organization of physical distribution within its own orbit. The marketing function, for example, may be asked to accept slower delivery times; this may present an obstacle to the fulfilment of the *other* goal of physical distribution — to enhance product sales, and thus contribute increased revenue, through offering an attractive order-cycle time.

Customer service

The final output of a total distribution system can be seen as *customer service*. Customer service is often defined as the service provided to the customer from the time an order is placed until the product is delivered. There are three key aspects to customer service:
1. availability of the product
2. completion of orders reliably and in good time
3. ease of communication and documentation.

Exercise: Think about this concept of customer service and its key elements for a moment. Do you think that providing customer service means maximizing all three key elements, all the time?

In fact, it is more appropriate to think of customer service as a variable standard or level which is to be aimed at — but not necessarily the maximum standard to be attained all the time. This is because providing customer service adds to costs as well as to revenue. Customers may have a clear idea of the standard of customer service they will accept, but it may not be the maximum possible if that turns out to be too expensive.

So you should think of the output of all distribution activity as the provision of a *consciously chosen standard* or level of customer service, bearing in mind costs and revenues — and therefore profit contribution (see Figure 16.6). As always, customer service is the ultimate goal. But it is a *relative* concept of customer service that is needed, not an absolute one.

In the next chapter, the tools and concepts examined here are put to use in developing the 'right' approach to distribution.

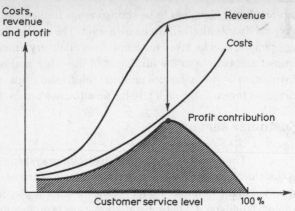

Figure 16.6.   The distribution efficiency–cost relationship

Checklist

Marketers should ensure that they know what is meant by:

trading versus physical aspects of distribution

a trading channel

intermediaries

channel power

channel structure

channel integration, both horizontal and vertical

the total distribution concept

customer service as a level or standard, not an absolute goal.

17 The 'Right' Place

Your place or mine?

As you will remember from the last two chapters, what we really want is to develop an approach to distribution that gives us the 'right' level of customer service – getting the right product to the right place at the right time. And you will remember that this involves the two different aspects (a) of making products available to buy, and (b) of making them physically available to the customer.

The 'right' place will, however, mean different things for different types of business. What does 'place' mean to the retailer? An important aspect of place will be the location of outlets to serve the final customers' needs. But a retailer also has to think about how stock will reach the outlet at the right time; so 'place' to a retailer also means the location of depots or distribution centres serving the retail outlet, how supplies will reach the outlet, and relationships with suppliers.

What does a manufacturer mean by 'place'? Being in a different position in the trading channel, the factors involved in getting the right product to the right place at the right time look rather different through the eyes of the manufacturer. A consumer goods manufacturer will be concerned that appropriate shops and retail outlets stock the product-lines and that they are well positioned within the store. Achievement of this dual goal will involve the manufacturer in forging good working relationships with intermediaries such as agents and wholesalers.

Whatever the type of business, though, there is no single right way of distributing a product. This is why two different manufacturers of the same product (or similar products) may choose different methods of distributing it.

Exercise: You may care to think of an example of a product you know something about, which is made by at least two different manufacturers. Do they distribute the product in the same way or have they chosen different routes?

Selecting the right method of distribution really means selecting the right marketing channel. And, while there is no uniformly correct channel of distribution, a range of factors exists which should always be taken into account in channel selection. The same range of factors can be used in evaluating channels already chosen. This chapter therefore will concentrate on examining the factors which are likely to determine the 'right' choice of channel.

Selecting the right channel

Figure 17.1 sets out the main steps involved in selecting a channel of distribution. In common with all logical sequential processes of this type, a prerequisite is a clear set of objectives and guidelines on policy. These distribution objectives will be implicit in the overall marketing and operations objectives and can normally be derived from these more global aims. Only with an understanding of what is to be achieved can attention be constructively focused on the ways and means.

In formulating the distribution objectives, it is important to keep

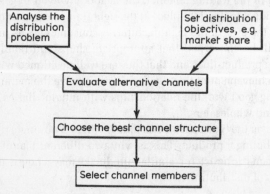

Figure 17.1.   Selecting the 'right' place

in mind that distribution is an integral part of the 'total offer'. This means that it has to be compatible with all the other elements of marketing, including product characteristics, price levels and promotional messages. It is essential too that the distribution network matches the requirements of the market-place.

Analysing the distribution problem

The nature of the distribution problem facing the company is defined by:

the market to be served

the characteristics of the product to be distributed

the kinds of channel used by competitors

the resources of the company itself.

Market characteristics

A fundamental influence on the nature and scope of distribution is the type of market the product is aimed at. For instance, if it is an industrial market with many people influencing the purchase decision, it may be worth employing a sales force and using direct distribution to ensure greater control over distribution to the company.

Exercise: Jot down some other influences which you think market type would have on channel selection.

The *size* of market is an important factor. In general, the larger the number of individual customers, the more likely it is that intermediaries will be useful. It is not only absolute market size that matters, though, because distribution methods must take account of how *concentrated* or *dispersed* the market population is in geographical terms. Usually, distribution becomes more difficult, the more dispersed the market; and so, in this case, intermediaries are more likely to be used.

The *sophistication* of the customers comprising a market also has a bearing on channel selection. The more informed and confident the customers, the more discerning they are likely to be – and the more critical of the service they receive through the selected distribution channel.

The how, when, where and who of purchasing are very important issues for a company when analysing the distribution options for its products. Decisions on channel structure, as with all decisions in marketing, should start with the customer and work back. Distribution should always be tailored to the way that customers actually buy the product in the market. For example, if customers buy a product in small lots, it is more likely to be worth while using intermediaries for their 'bulk-breaking' services. On the other hand, if customers like to shop from home, then perhaps mail order should be used.

Product characteristics

Exercise: What are the relevant product characteristics to look at, from the point of view of selecting a trading channel? Jot down what you think are the main factors to consider. Think about both trading and physical distribution factors.

Your list may include looking at whether a product is

> cheap or expensive
>
> perishable or durable
>
> technical or simple
>
> portable or needing installation
>
> in need of maintenance or not, and so on.

Exercise: Now spend a moment or two considering each product characteristic. Which characteristics do you think would suggest the use of:

(a) a long channel, that is one with several intermediaries?

(b) a short channel?

The sorts of characteristics which indicate long, indirect channels include cheap, standardized products and those without a very high technical content. Short and direct distribution channels are more suitable for perishable or expensive goods, custom-made goods, bulky and heavy goods which are relatively costly to move, and goods with a very high technical content meant for industrial markets.

As a useful generalization, it's worth remembering

> low turnover, high profit margin goods suit short trading channels
>
> high turnover, low profit margin goods suit longer trading channels.

Useful generalizations can be made too about the kinds of promotion suitable for each type of product; thus, a link can be made here with the question of the 'right' promotion. Products suited to short, direct channels are also suited to direct promotion. Products suited to longer, indirect channels are also suited to more indirect promotion, such as advertising on television and in the press.

Competition

As well as market and product characteristics, other factors enter into analysis of the distribution problem a company faces. One factor is the kinds of channel used by its *competitors* in the market. Many markets have long-established distribution patterns and norms which it is difficult for a single firm to overturn or ignore. This is the case with many pharmaceutical and chemical products, building supplies, and so on. On the other hand, in other markets competitors will each be using a different channel structure as a competitive tool, and some will be more successful than others.

Company resources and policies

A company analysing its distribution problem and selecting a suitable channel structure will also need to be aware of the limits set by the company's own *resources* and by its other *policies*. Some distribution options are available only to large companies with substantial financial resources. The expense of direct distribution in consumer markets, for instance, can usually be borne only by large firms with the necessary financial and managerial resources. Smaller producers will tend to lack both the capital and the distribution expertise necessary to make this a realistic option.

And, of course, the company's distribution policy must fit in with other aspects of company policy (such as capital investment policies) which will determine whether or not the company wants to invest in warehousing and vehicles.

Evaluating alternative channel structures and choosing 'the best'

Despite the generalizations that we have been able to make, it is very hard to prescribe in advance how a particular company should distribute a particular product – and how, in detail, it should set about making this choice.

Once the various factors involved in the company's distribution problem have been analysed, a *range* of possible distribution channel options should emerge. The next step should then be to compare the various channels that seem possible and to select one from among the range of possibilities. The selection of the 'best' channel among several then depends on a *value judgement* of the importance of all the various considerations.

Exercise: What criteria do you think will help the marketer's selection at this second stage?

As we saw in the last chapter, there are really two conflicting criteria at work in distribution decisions. From the physical distribution side especially, the company's own *cost* considerations must be one criterion. But, on the other hand, revenue considerations and therefore *customer service* must be another criterion. The choice is not simple.

Into the decision must also be fed the company's *distribution policy* priorities, which must fit in with other aspects of the marketing mix. The company must decide what degree of market coverage its distribution policy is aiming at. The channel selected should provide a firm with the ability to serve a predetermined share and sector of a market.

Market coverage can be intensive or selective – that is to say, the company can attempt blanket coverage of the whole market or can attempt to target its distribution more selectively on to specific segments of that market. At one extreme, the company may even attempt to become the exclusive supplier to some areas of the market. Channel selection will vary accordingly.

Finally, the external competitive environment must be taken into account in the attempt to see how the desired market coverage can be achieved. Are competitors using distribution channels as a very positive competitive tool? Are rapid changes taking place in the distribution of competitors' products?

Selecting channel members

Once the decision has been made as to the most appropriate channel structure, it is time to decide the nitty-gritty question of who the channel's members will be. Of course, if direct distribution is chosen, there are no channel members to select. Otherwise, selection of trading channel members and physical distribution channel members are both needed.

A useful 10-point checklist for a producer to go through when selecting channel members is:

1. credit and finance position
2. distributor's sales strength – numbers and competence
3. distributor's product-lines handled – competing and complementary product-lines
4. reputation

5. market coverage
6. sales performance
7. management ability
8. management succession and continuity
9. attitudes – enthusiasm and aggressiveness
10. size – organization and sales volume.

Exercise: Think of a product-line that you know well. Consider at
least two possible distributors for this product-line.
Which would you at first assume would do the best job,
and why? Now go through the checklist, point by point,
and see:

whether you change your choice

whether a decision is easier to make

whether you now have clearer reasons for your initial
choice.

It is important to remember that selection of channel members is not
a one-way process. Wholesalers and retailers want to choose whom
they represent, just as manufacturers want to choose who represents
them. To secure the services of good intermediaries, most producers
will have to 'sell' themselves to the distributors they have selected.
To do this, they may well stress the support which a producer can
offer to intermediaries. Inducements can include:

sales instruction

management aids

sales promotion/advertising

distributor advisory panels.

Evaluating channels

After a trading channel has been set up with a selected
structure and members, its working should periodically be reviewed
and evaluated. Most often in practice channel evaluation takes the

form of channel *member* evaluation only. As we remarked in the last chapter, producers often complain about their intermediaries' performance and the level of service they offer. It is not often that the channel *structure* as well as its members is re-evaluated to see whether *it* remains the 'best' option.

In practice also, evaluation of trading channels is usually a response to some specific problem. This could involve inroads into the market made by competitors; the appearance of a major new product; a notable change in costs; or a shift in consumer demand.

By contrast, we would stress that choosing the 'right' approach to distribution needs to be part of a regular and planned process, not just a 'panic' response to problems. Both channel structure and channel members' performance should be subject to regular review.

Sound evaluation of channel member performance requires carefully thought-out standards of criteria against which members are to be measured. Informal evaluation, without a clear set of criteria, usually gives biased results.

Some useful criteria for measuring channel member performance are:

> sales performance of channel members
>
> inventory maintained
>
> selling capabilities
>
> attitudes
>
> competition faced by channel members
>
> members' general growth prospects.

Exercise: Now look through this list again. Which criteria do you imagine are the most frequently used in practice?

Trading channel members tend to be evaluated on *sales performance*; *physical* distributors tend to be evaluated differently, and not by the above criteria at all – their performance tends to be measured on the basis of *cost*.

In carrying out a regular 'audit' of channel structures and members, every effort should be made to use a number of different criteria. No single criterion can provide a complete picture. Take sales performance, for example. Below-average sales could be due to the weather or to poor supplies – both factors outside the control of the channel member. So, in these cases, poor sales performance of that one channel member does *not* indicate that the member is a 'weak link' in the chain, and should be replaced.

Checklist

The 'right' approach to place involves:

selecting the best trading channel

securing the best channel members

regular and systematic re-evaluation.

Factors to look at in channel selection include:

market characteristics

product characteristics

competitor channels

company resources and policies.

Selecting the 'best' channel needs a value judgement, arrived at as a result of weighing up these various factors.

The processes of choosing channel members and then of assessing their performance should be done against a range of criteria, not just according to one rule of thumb.

18 Price as a Market Offering

What is the customer paying for?

Exercise: Imagine for a moment a situation in which you are sufficiently interested in a product to inquire as to its price.
On learning the amount involved, your response is, 'It's
too expensive.' Jot down some notes on what exactly you
might *mean* by that statement. Would it be likely to indicate, for example, that you simply do not have enough
money to pay the asking price? Or does the statement
convey something else about your attitude to the product
in question?

Now imagine yourself in the same situation – but this
time with the difference that your reaction on learning the
price of the product is, 'Well, that's good value.' Once
again, jot down some notes on what you might mean by
that statement.

The 'price' element of the marketing mix, you may conclude rue-
fully, is just as complicated as either 'product' or 'place'. You would
be right to come to this conclusion – but, in fact, relatively few
organizations make sophisticated use of this element of the mar\-
ing mix. In most organizations, price is arrived at by a blend of cost
accounting (that is, calculating what costs are involved in *producing*
the product) and guesswork as to what the market will bear, one of
the main reference points being the kind of prices set by the competition.

Why is it that price receives so little creative marketing attention?
Part of the reason is that there is often considerable confusion over
what the concept of price actually means in a marketing context.
Traditionally, economic theory has been the framework for thinking
about price; and this type of theory, though helpful in some ways,

has only a limited use in unravelling the complexities associated with pricing for the market-place.

In its simplest expression, economic theory presents price, value and utility as related concepts. *Utility* is that attribute of an item which makes it capable of satisfying wants. *Value* is the quantitative expression of the power a product has to attract other products in exchange. In a barter system, for example, the value of product X (a certain amount of grain, say) may be reckoned in terms of a standard amount of product Y (livestock, let us say). Since we use money as a common denominator of value, the term 'price' is employed to describe the money value of an item. *Price* is value expressed in terms of whatever the monetary medium may be in the country where the exchange takes place.

Problems of definition arise, however, when the attempt is made to make a direct comparison between prices and products. Let us suppose that William has paid £10 to send an urgent package, in the course of which he had himself to arrange for its delivery to a railway station; conversely, Julia paid only £1.75 for sending her package, and she could take it to a dispatch point very convenient to her. And let us suppose also that the price quoted to William for a garden shed was £1000, while Julia paid only £250.

At first glance, Julia may look like the winner (better business person?) in both cases. However, other factors are involved which may qualify this judgement. In the first example, William's priorities were that his package should arrive safely and on time – and that, if this failed to happen, he should be able to claim adequate compensation. Julia had the same concern that her package should arrive on time; but, by using a less reliable service which, in addition, did not offer any compensation if the package failed to arrive in time, she failed to protect her interests if things went wrong.

In the second case, William had the shed delivered to his address and erected in his garden for him, giving him immediate use of it. He also arranged to pay for the shed in monthly instalments. Julia paid in cash for a partially assembled shed, arranged for its delivery herself, and over the next few months spent rather more time than she had intended in completing the structure and making it ready for use.

Exercise: The question now must be asked again: who paid the
                higher price for their product?

Whatever your answer, the moral is clear enough. Many variables
are involved in defining price as a market offering, and the final
arbiters of 'value for money' are individual customers.   Central to
assessing the position of price in the marketing mix is an accurate
identification of exactly what it is that the customer is buying. Chapter 11, you may remember, discussed how products can usefully be
seen in terms of the various benefits they bring to customers. As
we have seen, customers normally buy much more than a physical
product alone; the seller therefore must take these 'extra', value-
adding factors into account in setting a price on the product.

Price and the 'total offer'

Further implications flow from this. Since the customer
is buying the 'total offer' presented by the company, the price put on
the product must also be appropriate to the 'place' and 'promotion'
elements of the particular marketing mix involved. Effective marketing strategy depends on the 'price' element being seen as an integral
part of the 'total offer', dovetailing with the other elements to
comprise a coherent and clearly targeted market offering.

Let us examine for a moment just what might be involved in ensuring that the price is consistent with the other elements of the mix.
Take the channels of distribution, for example. A manufacturer's
price for his product will depend partly on the channels selected
and the types of intermediaries involved. A firm selling both through
wholesalers and directly to retailers, for instance, will often offer its
product at a different price to each of these two groups of customers.
And this price will, of course, reflect the different 'total offer' available to each of the customer groups. These 'total offers' may differ
in terms of, for example, quantities supplied, delivery schedules,
packaging and promotional support.

Exercise: Go back for a moment to our earlier example of the garden
                shed and think about the two 'total offers' involved in

terms of value for money. Try to construct separate marketing arguments which would be likely to appeal first to customers like William and then to customers like Julia. Now compare your thoughts with ours, given below.

The 'William' customer:

Our sheds offer busy people the satisfaction of top-quality workmanship in both construction and installation.

You won't have to bother with making complicated arrangements. Our people will arrive and install the shed in a single afternoon (or morning or evening – at your convenience). *And* they'll clear up the mess after them. What's more, we'll give you six months to pay, with interest-free credit.

We're not in the DIY business. Our customers are concerned about quality and are willing to employ professionals to get the job done.

The 'Julia' customer:

Why pay a fortune for a shed?

You can buy our self-assembly units with easy-to-follow instructions and have the satisfaction that can only come from DIY – and all at a fraction of the ready-made price.

Perhaps you've always wanted a shed but it was beyond your reach? Now you can afford one *and* have the satisfaction of helping to create it.

Price and quality

Price, then, is an integral part of the 'total offer', contributing to the customer's perception of the benefits offered by the product itself. At times, price may even be seen as a benefit itself.

Exercise: Can you think of some examples of buying situations in which the price of the product might itself be seen as a benefit? In formulating your examples, have you made the assumption that only a *low* price could be perceived to provide benefits?

In fact, in different circumstances, both high and low levels of price can be perceived as conferring benefits. Few customers, for example, would be willing to believe that, in normal circumstances, a bottle of 'good' perfume could be acquired for a low price. With perfume, a premium price is itself an important part of the purchase.

No marketing executive should forget that, for many other products as well as perfume, consumers tend to associate higher quality with higher price. This association is most common in two particular types of situation:

> where consumers must make purchase decisions but have incomplete information on the different options available to them; that is, in situations where price is virtually the only clue as to product quality

> where products are likely to enhance an individual's social 'image' if they are seen to be 'expensive'.

Consumers' perception of quality, of course, can also be influenced by the reputation of the firm that makes the product, the store that sells it and the degree and type of advertising used to promote it. Indeed, factors such as these are usually needed to *support* the premium price charged.

However, it should be noted that research tells us that products with the leading market share tend *not* to be the cheapest available – despite their high volume sales. Low prices are not normally the key to the success of brand leaders. Leading products benefit instead from being perceived as comprising the most satisfactory 'total offer' available; in other words, they present the best 'value for money'. This result often owes much to the formulation of a marketing mix that focuses on quality and value – and does not apologize for the price.

Checklist

> In considering price as a market offering, organizations should:

> analyse price as a market variable in the same way as the other elements of the marketing mix

make an accurate identification of what it is the customer is being asked to pay for

ensure that the 'price' element of the mix dovetails with the other elements to comprise a coherent 'total offer'

bear in mind the association commonly made between price and quality.

19 Pricing Tools and Techniques

Who chooses the tools?

It is sometimes said that 'most accountants will enable a company to save money, but few will create the situation for making money'. Many marketers would argue that, when it comes to pricing decisions, this statement holds a great deal of truth.

Within any organization there are a number of different parties who want to influence the pricing decision. Each will put forward sound arguments designed to safeguard their own department's interests – and, as they see it, the interests of the company as a whole. But, in the final analysis, the price level will be aimed at covering costs and making a reasonable profit. Since pricing is about money, and since money is fundamental to a company's existence, the person whose influence may be greatest is the accountant.

Strong influence from the accountancy side can be seen clearly reflected in the cost-based pricing methods employed by many organizations. However, the pervasiveness of cost-based pricing is not due solely to the influence of accountants. The method appeals to businessmen in general because it looks scientific, logical and based on fact.

We go on now to take a brief look at some of the cost-based methods; and we shall then explore some alternative, market-based methods of pricing.

Cost-based methods of pricing
Cost plus

In its simplest form, the cost-plus approach means that the selling price for a unit of a product is equal to the product's total cost, plus an amount to cover the anticipated profit on the unit. This generally means that the selling price is derived from three main elements:

> direct costs
>
> allocation of overheads
>
> percentage profit contribution.

At first glance, this method of pricing seems to have a lot in its favour. It ensures, for example, that a profit is made on each item sold. Importantly, too, it is an easy system to operate. Since all organizations keep cost information, all that is required to determine the price is a simple calculation based on the cost accounts.

However, there are drawbacks to this method which seriously undermine its value as a pricing tool. First of all, few organizations are in a position to produce adequate and accurate cost data. Direct costs (for example, those involved in buying materials and labour) can be measured relatively accurately; but it is virtually impossible for most organizations to measure individual products' share of indirect costs and general overheads. This usually means that these costs are spread across all products by a percentage allocation which may or may not reflect the true share of the costs incurred by individual products. Added to this is the fact that accountants normally base their cost calculations on sales forecasts – that is, projections of future sales – rather than on actual sales. At the end of the day, despite the appearance of incorporating scientific 'truth', most cost calculations present little more than a very approximate picture of what the product costs the company to produce.

The second main drawback to this method of pricing is perhaps even more serious. As we saw in the previous chapter, it is essential that the price of a product should make sense in terms of the expectations of the market-place. But how can this happen (except by chance) if the customer's viewpoint is ignored when the price is set? The customer is interested in price as a user, not as a manufacturer. The cost of production is a matter of total indifference to customers; instead, they are interested in the benefits associated with the product and the value that they put on those benefits. Customers therefore set their own 'market value' on a product by evaluating the benefits associated with it and comparing them with those offered by competing products. That assessment is then translated into a reckoning of the price the customer would be willing to pay for the product.

Exercise: Can you think of a situation in which you felt that the price put on a product was quite wrong for the intended target market? In your opinion, was the price too high or too low? What effect do you suspect that this price level was having on sales? Do you think it likely that the organization had taken market factors into account in setting the price?

Break-even analysis

Although it differs from cost-plus pricing in that it does to some extent take market demand into account, break-even analysis is essentially another tool for cost-based pricing.

A break-even analysis involves developing tables and charts, such as Figure 19.1, to help an organization determine at what level of output revenues will equal costs – assuming a certain selling price. At levels above the break-even point, sales will result in a profit on

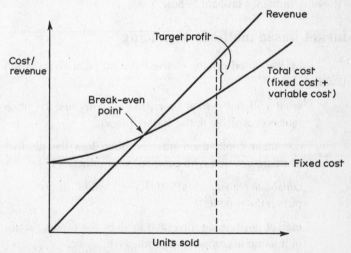

Figure 19.1.   Break-even analysis

each unit; the further above the break-even point sales go, the higher will be the total and unit profits. Sales below the break-even point will result in a loss to the seller.

The main drawbacks to this method are as follows:

> it assumes that costs per unit are static

> it ignores the fact that revenue will be affected by price; that is, that different price levels will themselves affect market demand.

Despite these drawbacks, break-even analysis can serve as a valuable aid in price decisions, particularly for firms which exist in a situation of reasonably stable costs and demand structures. However, the fact that many of the underlying assumptions are unrealistic in a practical business operation means that this method is most useful when used as an analytical tool in conjunction with other pricing techniques.

Before going on to consider market-based approaches to pricing, it's worth pointing out that most critics of cost-based pricing do not take the view that costs should be disregarded altogether. Costs should exert *an* influence on price, they argue – but they should not be the *only* influence brought to bear.

Market-based methods of pricing

Market-based pricing concentrates on an analysis of the following areas:

> what will the market bear (that is, what are the price ranges acceptable to the market-place)?

> consumer comparison (that is, how does the product compare in value with competitive products?)

> consumer expectations (that is, what 'value' do customers put on the product?)

> market positioning (that is, how does the product stand in relation to competitive products?)

Let us examine two of these factors in rather more detail.

Pricing for 'value'

As we have seen, in the customers' eyes, price is related to the value
of the product in use rather than to the cost of manufacture. Most
customers will have a predetermined (although often unconscious)
'value for money' checklist; and even if the product offers benefits
wholly relevant to the customer, the 'wrong' price may well jeopard-
ize the sale.

We have seen too that the 'wrong' price is not necessarily a high
price. Since many customers make an association between price
and quality, setting a low price on a product which carries 'quality'
connotations may seriously damage sales. Let us examine a situation
of this kind in rather more detail. A price is set on a new DIY decorating aid on the basis of direct costs, plus a contribution to overheads
and profit; in fact, this price is considerably lower than that which
the customer is willing to pay. The result is that the customer puts
the decorating aid into the 'useless gimmick, not worth a try'
category. Consequently, the manufacturer suffers lost revenue and,
perhaps even more importantly, lost market position.

Any system of market-based pricing must obviously explore in
some detail what constitutes 'value' in the customer's eyes. The
influences on this perception will vary from market to market, but
are likely to include one or more of the following:

> disposable income available
>
> urgency of need
>
> comparison with competitive offerings
>
> seasonal factors (for example, 'out of season' holiday
> bargains)
>
> trends and fashions (that is, how important it is to the
> customer to buy immediately)
>
> importance put on prompt delivery and after-sales service
>
> importance put on reliability and quality of the product
> itself.

Marketing research is often needed to identify exactly which factors are important in any given market. Getting to know customers and their requirements is at least as important as establishing what product features and benefits are desirable.

Pricing to meet competition

When setting prices, it is prudent for a company to take account of the price levels imposed by its major competitors. Intense and aggressive competitive activity may depress the selling price of competing products, whereas a few comfortable and cosy competitors may mean higher selling prices.

A company may reduce its prices to below the competitive norm in order to gain an increased market share. However, if its competitors decide to meet this price, then the company may find itself in a vulnerable situation – especially if it is smaller or financially weaker than the competition. The lower prices leave less money to spend on marketing activities to counter the increased competition at the lower price. The result may be that the firm finds itself with only the same, or even a reduced, market share; at the same time, because of the lower prices, it will be receiving lower returns from its sales.

In many markets, a dominant market leader will virtually dictate price levels. Firms tend to be either 'price makers' or 'price takers'.

Let us now take a look at how a firm can apply the principles of market-based pricing in practice.

Company A developed a product in the field of light engineering. A high market demand for the product type was reflected in strong and aggressive competition. Company A's product was characterized by several unique characteristics which offered significant improved customer benefits. In addition, Company A developed a manufacturing and product assembly process which offered considerable saving in production costs.

A cost-plus approach to pricing yielded a figure considerably lower than that of the nearest competition. Market research, however, revealed that at this price customers did not believe that the product would really provide the additional benefits promised. Company A therefore decided to take a market-based approach to pricing. Accordingly, the product was priced at a level at which customers believed that it could indeed be expected to offer the additional benefits; this price was 5 per cent above the nearest competition.

The product proved to be a continued success over a number of years; and an 'added value' price (incorporating modifications and extras) subsequently rose significantly higher than that of the nearest competition.

Discounts and allowances

We have looked at the following influences on the final selling price of a product:

manufacturing costs

customers' perceptions of value

pressure from competitors.

We now turn to consider another important influence: that of the chain of distribution involved in getting the product to the final user. Having set the basic (list) price, the manufacturer must next decide what kind of discount schedule to adopt. Discounts and allowances to retailers, wholesalers and other intermediaries result in deductions from the list price. These deductions may be in the form of cash or some other concession, such as a free case of merchandise. The main types of discount in common use are as follows:

Quantity discounts

These deductions from list prices are offered by sellers in order to:

encourage customers to buy in larger amounts. Thus, customers may be offered a discount if they make an individual order for a certain amount of product.

tie the customer to the seller. Thus, discounts are based on the total volume purchased over a period of time.

The discounts may be based either on monetary value or on quantity of goods purchased.

Trade discounts

These discounts form a reduction in the list price offered to buyers in payment for marketing and selling activities which they will undertake for the product.

Cash discounts

A cash discount is a deduction granted to buyers for paying their bills within a specified period of time.

Other forms of discount

If the supplier produces a product, such as holidays, which are purchased on a seasonal basis, management may feel it appropriate to offer *seasonal discounts*. These are discounts of, say, 5, 10 or 20 per cent which are given to customers during slack periods to encourage purchase. The same principle lies behind the decision by telephone companies to vary their charges according to the time of day a call is made.

Promotional allowances are discounts granted by suppliers for promotional support provided by re-sellers. For example, a drinks manufacturer may offer a retailer a free case for every dozen sold if the retailer undertakes to reduce retail selling prices by a specified amount and feature the special offer in local press advertising.

Checklist

In deciding which pricing methods are appropriate to its circumstances, the organization should:

weigh up the advantages and disadvantages of a cost-based approach

assess the potential value of a market-based approach

identify the market features which are most relevant to pricing decisions (for example, do the organization's customers make a quality/value association?)

develop a system for discounts and allowances which is satisfactory both to the organization and to members of the distribution chain.

20 The 'Right' Price

What is a price meant to do?

Discussion of the 'right' price can perhaps begin most usefully by exploring what is indubitably the 'wrong' price for any product. A price can be perceived to be 'wrong' when:

> the price charged for the product is consistently and unintentionally at a level below what the product costs to produce. In this situation, the business is unlikely to survive for long

> it falls significantly above or below the perceived value of the product to potential purchasers. In this situation, the product's intended market may disappear or change.

Pricing levels therefore must normally be set somewhere between (a) what the product costs to make and sell, and (b) the upper parameter of its value to the customer.

In the last two chapters we looked at some of the different influences in the market-place which affect the final selling price.

Exercise: Take a moment now to recollect and jot down what some of these influences are. If you find difficulty in remembering more than one or two, glance back through Chapters 18 and 19.

Let us now turn to an examination of how an organization can proceed to develop pricing policies which ensure that the price element of the 'total offer' is consistent with, and contributes to, the overall marketing objectives for the product.

First of all, the most important thing is that the organization should be clear as to what role pricing is supposed to play in its overall marketing strategies. This means developing clear *pricing objectives*.

Pricing objectives

Unless clear objectives are developed, the organization will find itself being forced to respond randomly to the pricing moves of its competitors. Among the many forms that these objectives can take, the following are the most common:

to achieve target return on investment or on net sales. Many retailers and wholesalers seek a certain percentage return on *net sales* as a pricing objective in the short term. Firms which are leaders in their industry typically select as an objective a target return on *investment*.

to stabilize prices. The goal of stabilizing prices is often found in industries where demand can fluctuate frequently and which is dominated by large companies.

to gain or improve market share. Especially in times of increasing markets, market share is often a much more desirable goal than target return on investment.

to meet or prevent competition. A seller may price to discourage some competitors and forestall others from entering the market.

to maximize profit over the longer term. The long-term maximizing of profits may require a firm to accept low profits, and even losses, in the short term. It may be desirable, for example, for a firm to price low on some products in the short term in order to build market share or to undermine, or even remove, the competition.

Having decided on its pricing objectives, the organization must then proceed to identify the *pricing strategies* which are most likely to enable it to meet these objectives.

Pricing strategies

Particularly in the early stages of a product's life-cycle, marketers must select one of two choices of strategy:

pricing high in order to maximize the unit contribution

pricing low in order to maximize unit volume and forestall competition.

The former strategy is usually known as *price skimming*, the latter as *penetration pricing*.

Price skimming

A skimming strategy involves setting a price which is high in the range of prices expected by the market-place. The seller may continue with this strategy for an indefinite period or, after a certain period of time, may decide to lower the price in order to gain access to other segments of the market.

Through pursuing this strategy, the organization can reach those customers who respond to distinctiveness and exclusiveness in a product and who are relatively insensitive to price. This may result not only in maximum short-term revenue gains but also in the development of a 'prestige' image for the product – an image which may serve the product well even after the price has been reduced.

The first manufacturers of the pocket calculator used a price-skimming strategy to good effect. High prices reflected the 'value-added' component of these new examples of high technology; and the market was happy to pay the price. Once the competition intensified, the first manufacturers brought down their prices to match those of the new entrants, and then went on to participate in the 'saturation' of the market-place. The manufacturers of other consumer durables – such as telephone answering machines – have employed similar strategies.

Many organizations find that a 'skimming' strategy is particularly suitable for new products which enjoy a high degree of *differentiation*. This simply means that the product has one or more unique characteristics which differentiate it from competing products.

These characteristics will frequently involve attributes of the product itself, such as that it lasts longer, offers more convenience, and so on. At times, however, the differentiating factor may be that the product is aimed at a particular market niche which has not, as yet, been explored by the organization's competitors.

The reasons for the desirability of a skimming policy in these circumstances include:

> the ability to make the most of the lack of competition in the market-place
>
> in the event of a miscalculation in setting a price, the relative ease of lowering (as opposed to raising) that price
>
> the use of high prices to keep demand within the limits of the company's ability to produce the product.

Penetration pricing

In this strategy, a low initial price is set in order to gain immediate access to the mass market. It is often employed in the following circumstances:

> where the price of the product has an extremely important influence on market demand
>
> where substantial savings in production and marketing costs can be achieved through large-scale operations
>
> where the product is likely to face very strong competition
>
> where the product has little or no differentiation
>
> where market share is a prime objective.

A good example of a product priced at a level aimed at penetrating the market is provided by the Amstrad personal computer. While its capabilities may not be exactly the same as those of other personal computers, the price is considerably lower than that of the competition. The effect of this price is to stimulate interest from a large section of consumers who previously would have considered a personal computer beyond their economic reach. As a result of its pricing strategy, Amstrad has penetrated the market and achieved a substantial market share.

Modifying the strategies

There are many variations on skimming and penetration strategies. In 'prestige' pricing, for example, the objective is to create a prestige image for the product by offering it at a price which implies that it is exclusively up-market. On the other hand, a 'bargain pricing' strategy may be used to stimulate quick demand and return on revenue. This strategy may be employed as a shorter-term option than penetration pricing.

Sometimes particular circumstances prevailing in an industry may require particular pricing strategies. For example, a manufacturer may be faced with considerable fluctuations in the price of raw materials. If these fluctuations were to be reflected in the final selling price of the product, the manufacturer's customers would be confronted with widely varying prices. In these circumstances, it may be desirable for the manufacturer to establish a 'plateau' pricing strategy, by which his selling price is stabilized at a level which can take account of the fluctuations. Sometimes substantial losses may have to be carried; but these are likely to be offset by larger profits at other times (see Figure 20.1).

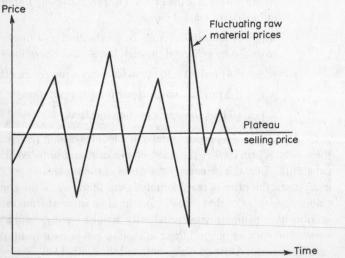

Figure 20.1.   Plateau pricing

Competitive pricing

Useful though they are in the right circumstances, neither skimming nor penetration strategies provide the complete answer to a firm's pricing problems.

Exercise: Can you suggest some reasons why many organizations find (a) a skimming strategy, and (b) a penetration strategy inappropriate to their circumstances?

You'll probably have noted down, quite rightly, that both these strategies are designed to meet 'extreme' circumstances: in the first case, a product has a considerable degree of exclusivity; in the second, a truly mass market is involved. In fact, of course, most products fit into the vast middle band of the price continuum. Producers find it difficult to achieve sufficient differentiation to allow successful skimming pricing; and, in addition, many producers have insufficient resources to finance a penetration pricing policy. As a result, most products are hemmed in by many close direct and indirect competitors.

The pricing strategy employed in this situation is that known as 'what the market will bear', or 'competitive' pricing. This strategy dictates that the product be priced in relation *both* to the competition *and* to customer perceptions of value for money.

Exercise: Think back to what you learned about market pricing in the last chapter. Can you remember the main factors that need to be taken into account when setting price according to this method? Re-read the relevant section if you cannot remember what these factors are.

The companies which are most successful in using competitive pricing are those which have made a careful analysis of the different market factors involved – and which have gone on to fine-tune their price levels accordingly.

Selecting the 'right' strategy

Exercise: What guidelines can the organization use in deciding which pricing strategy is most appropriate to its particular circumstances?

As we have seen, the central consideration is to set the right objectives for the market circumstances; and these circumstances, it should be remembered, may be influenced substantially by long-established customer expectations or by the very nature of the competition. Particularly where it finds itself in the competitive pricing band, the organization must be careful to assess all the factors relevant to determining its pricing strategy.

Thinking 'total offer'

The overriding consideration in setting prices, then, is the value of the product to the market. But it should be recognized that the customer's perception of an acceptable price may be strongly influenced by the 'total offer' available to him or her.

The 'right' price is one which is not only acceptable to the market

PRICE CONTINUUM		
low		high
	PRODUCT	
undifferentiated	– Design/appearance/style	differentiated
low	– Quality	high
intensive	DISTRIBUTION	exclusive
poor	– Reliability /availability	good
	PROMOTION	
little	– Activity	much
poor	IMAGE	good

NOTE : The above are only general tendencies. The exceptions prove the rule

Figure 20.2.   Integrating price with the total offer

but which is also totally integrated with the rest of the marketing elements (see Figure 20.2).

Thus, the price must reflect the characteristics of:

the *product* – in terms of the product's quality of materials and performance; its design and appearance and style; and its prestige and exclusivity or otherwise

the *distribution* – in terms of the availability and reliability of supply; and the intensiveness or selectiveness of distribution

the *promotion* – in terms of its levels of intensity and activity; its selectivity and targeting

the *image* – in terms of all the factors described above.

A successful total integration depends on marketing management's ability to pay full attention to detail and leave nothing to chance. The 'right' price can be arrived at only through a process of evaluation of market factors and co-ordinated planning of the marketing effort. And it should be remembered that, difficult and time-consuming though this process may be, it is by no means the end of the matter. Once the right price *has* been determined, hard-pressed marketing management must be prepared constantly to undertake the fine-tuning required to keep up with the dynamic movements of the market-place.

Checklist

In determining the 'right' price for its products, the organization should:

aim to set pricing levels somewhere between (a) what the product costs to make and sell, and (b) the upper parameter of its value to the customer

develop clear pricing objectives

proceed to identify the pricing strategies which will allow it to meet these objectives

consider the relevance to its market offering of:
- a price-skimming strategy
- a penetration pricing strategy
- competitive pricing

select a pricing level which is not only acceptable to the market but which is totally integrated with the other elements of the marketing mix

fine-tune pricing levels as market changes dictate.

21 Promotion as a Market Offering

What is promotion, anyway?

The 'promotion' element of the marketing mix may well be the one most familiar to you, both as a customer and as a marketer.

Exercise: Take a moment now to jot down the kind of activities which you believe are covered by the term 'promotion'.

You'll probably have included advertising, sales promotion and personal selling. But what about direct mail, sponsorship and public relations? And where do communications like letter headings, van signwriting and inquiry services fit into the picture?

As we shall see, the 'promotion' element of the mix covers all these aspects of marketing activity – and many more. But, in marketing shorthand, 'promotion' also covers other types of communication which are less directly within the organization's control. Customers and potential customers constantly pick up messages about an organization. Some of these messages are of the type mentioned above – that is, they come from sources within the organization's control. Others, however, are subject to much less direct influence by the organization. Word of mouth – the process through which customers influence the attitudes of potential customers – is an outstanding example of this indirect type of communication.

'Promotion', then, should be viewed as the *sum total of all the marketing communications associated with the firm* – including those communications which are not directly within the firm's control.

Another important point must be made here. Used in isolation from the other elements of the mix, promotion does *not* constitute 'marketing'. Why bother to mention this seemingly obvious point?

Quite simply, the need stems from the fact that many organizations – and smaller firms in particular – tend to pick on promotion as the most easily recognized aspect of marketing and proceed to deploy promotional activities without first analysing the whole marketing picture. Almost invariably, the result is that these organizations achieve much poorer results than they had anticipated.

Why is this? First of all, of course, neglect of the other components of the 'total offer' means that customers may well be disappointed in what they are actually being offered. The product may not be exactly what they want, for example; or it may not be easily available to them; or the price may not represent what they perceive to be value for money.

But, secondly, failure to probe into market conditions is likely to sabotage the promotional effort itself. Only an extraordinary run of luck can save a promotional campaign where the firm does not have a clear idea of:

> what, specifically, the campaign is intended to achieve
>
> what customers want from the products and services
>
> who the customers and potential customers are, and where they can be found.

The answers to these questions all constitute essential background information for a successful promotional campaign. After all, if you don't know who your customers are and where they can be found, how do you know how to contact them and where to advertise? And if you don't really understand what customers are looking for when they buy your type of product or service, how will you know what message to convey to attract the attention and interest of your audience? Finally, if you don't have clear objectives for your individual promotional efforts (that together make up your whole promotional campaign), how will you know if you have met these objectives?

Promotion and advertising are only a part, albeit an important part, of marketing. As such, they can only be truly effective when used in a co-ordinated fashion as an integral part of the total marketing effort.

Given that all the messages about the organization and its products cannot be controlled, it is important to ensure that those messages that *can* be controlled are sent to the right people in the best way to convey the most appropriate impression. It is important too that the organization does all it can to influence communications that cannot be controlled. A policy of keeping existing customers satisfied, for example, is likely to pay dividends in the way of positive word-of-mouth communications to potential customers.

Promotion is concerned with showing that what the organization produces matches what the customer wants. It is to do with closing the gap in perception between the way customers see the organization and the way the organization would like to be seen.

The nature – and the importance – of the promotional element of the mix can be illustrated by an examination of the old adage, 'the man who produces a better mousetrap will have people beat a path to his door'.

Exercise: Assume for a moment that there is a *need* for a better mousetrap and take a moment to think about this saying. Is it true, do you think? Will the invention of a clever new product automatically lead to rocketing sales?

The answer, of course, is that no, this will *not* happen automatically. Unless the mousetrap is *promoted* properly, the path to the door will remain quite unbeaten. There are several missing links in the saying as it stands:

1. How would people know that the man had a better mousetrap?
2. How would they know where to find him?
3. How would they know what makes his mousetrap 'better' – and what 'better' means in terms of the benefits they could expect from it?

Communications aims and objectives

Obviously, before any decisions can be made on promotional materials and methods, the marketer must know precisely what role he or she wants promotion to play in the marketing effort overall.

The overall aims of promotion – or 'persuasive communication', as some prefer to call it – can be summarized into the following steps:

> to arrest the *attention* of customers and potential customers in such a way that they become aware of the existence of the organization and its products
>
> to get customers *interested* in the organization and its products
>
> to create a *desire* to purchase
>
> to prompt the *action* of buying.

You may find the following tip useful in remembering these four stages: the acronym AIDA is formed from the initial letter of the four vital elements: **A**ttention, **I**nterest, **D**esire, **A**ction.

In some cases, marketers will be able to use the same communication to achieve all four aims. For example, in selling 'off the page' – that is, through the use of advertisements in newspapers with order coupons attached – a marketer will hope to take the reader through all four stages in quick succession, culminating in the newspaper reader's completion and dispatch of the order coupon.

More frequently, however, a marketer will find it necessary to plan different communication strategies to achieve each of the four aims. Take, for instance, a publisher promoting a potential bestseller to the book trade. The publisher might begin by arresting booksellers' *attention* through 'teasing' advertisements in the trade and national press. Nearer the time of the book's launch, he might go on to provoke further *interest* by ensuring that interviews with the author appear in the relevant magazines and papers. The booksellers' *desire to purchase* would then be stimulated by persuasive visits from the publisher's salesforce who would promise all kinds of sales aids – such as posters, counter packs and the like – and point to the money to be made by featuring the book in this way. At the same time, their visits would aim to prompt *action*, since the ultimate aim of the sales representative is to take an order.

Generally speaking, individual promotional campaigns are usually geared to take potential customers through only one or two of the decision-making steps implicit in AIDA. For example, they may aim to arrest attention and arouse interest; or they may aim to shift the desire to buy to the actual action of buying. It is worth noting here that the 'gap' between these last two steps (desire and action) is perhaps the greatest challenge facing the marketing communicator.

Exercise:　Think of a product or a service which you paid for recently. How were you persuaded to move from 'desire' to 'action'? Now think of a product which you thought of buying but in the end failed to do so. What kind of persuasion could the marketer have used to move you from 'desire' to 'action'?

Specific promotional strategies

Overall aims alone are not sufficient to enable the marketer to develop promotional strategies. They provide guidance but they do not indicate what precisely has to be achieved in order that the aims will be met. For this purpose, precise and specific objectives are needed. It is common for these objectives to cover, or be concerned with, the following:

> informing people about the organization's existence
>
> educating people about the organization's product range
>
> announcing a new product or service
>
> reminding people about the organization's existence
>
> persuading people that they should use the organization's products
>
> prompting action through a direct sale
>
> differentiating between the organization and its competitors
>
> image building
>
> influencing attitudes

> reinforcing the customer's decision to buy the
> organization's product
>
> explaining a new pricing structure.

In order to meet any of the aims and objectives mentioned so far,
any promotion must have:

> *impact*: in order to arrest attention
>
> *interest*: to retain attention
>
> *information*: to maintain attention and keep the audience
> reading/viewing.

The communication process

> What is involved in the process of communication?

Exercise: Take a moment now to jot down what you believe to be
the main components involved.

You'll probably find that your answers approximate to the following
description:

Source of the message: this is the organization or person who has
something they want to say.

Message: this refers to what is said. With promotion, the nature
of the message will relate back to the marketing communications
objectives selected as the most appropriate. Thus, where the objective is to differentiate between the organization and its competitors,
the message chosen to convey this might be, 'We offer an unusually
high standard of customer service.' It is important to remember that
a promotional message is by no means always one of 'Buy more'.

Media: this covers the various types of communication channel
available to transmit the message. In marketing, these might include

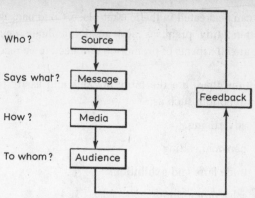

Figure 21.1.   The communications process

sales interviews, television commercials, press advertising, direct mail, and so on.

Audience: this refers to the receivers of the message. The communication cannot proceed to a successful conclusion unless the sender of the message has a very clear idea of who the communication is aimed at. In marketing communications, the audience will usually be a market segment. Successful communication depends largely on the compatibility of both message and medium with the expectations of the audience. In other words, every effort must be made to ensure that the form and content of the communication are likely to strike a receptive chord in the selected audience.

Figure 21.1 illustrates this process of communication – with the addition of an essential feedback loop between audience and source. Only if such feedback is available will the organization be able to modify its messages in line with customer response.

Methods of promotion and the promotional mix

As we have seen, the term 'promotion' embraces all tools which have persuasive communication as a major part of their role. That is, promotion covers all the different ways in which a favourable attitude towards the organization, along with its products and services, can be created in the market-place. Good packaging, well-typed letters, tidy premises and good telephone manners, for example, are all aspects of promotion and need to be recognized as such.

In addition, there are the more obvious and easily recognized forms of promotion, such as:

> advertising
>
> personal selling
>
> trade fairs and exhibitions
>
> sales promotions
>
> public relations
>
> sponsorship (as in, for example, the sponsorship of sporting events)
>
> point-of-sale promotion (the customer usually experiences this in the form of product packs, the way products are arranged and displayed, in-store promotional leaflets, and so on)
>
> direct mail (here the customer receives a personalized promotional letter, usually enclosing a leaflet or brochure)
>
> corporate logo/identity (customers are 'trained' to recognize such factors as store design, signwriting on vehicles, letter headings, and so on).

The way in which the different methods of communication are brought into play with one another to achieve the various objectives set for the promotional activity is usually referred to as the *promotional mix*. Putting together a promotional mix is rather like doing a jigsaw puzzle. Each piece has to fit in with every other piece – yet it has a significance of its own and a particular role to play.

The next chapter will look in some detail at the different promotional tools and how they can be used. For the moment, some examples may help to indicate the kind of role different methods of communication may play in the overall communications effort:

direct mail letters may be used to persuade the potential customer to agree to a sales visit

personal selling may be used to achieve a sale

television advertising may be used to inform a mass audience that a product exists which offers some new and worthwhile benefits

point-of-sale material may be used to encourage 'impulse buying'

competitions involving the collection of labels or coupons may be used to encourage customers to use a product on an extensive trial basis.

Who is the audience?

As we saw in Chapter 6, the immediate customer for any product or service is very often not the only person involved in the decision to buy. This customer is most probably a member of a formal or informal decision-making unit (DMU). When considering their audience, therefore, marketing communicators must make the identification of the DMUs operating in their market a matter of prime importance.

The members of these DMUs are the people who influence or decide upon the use of the organization's products or services. Accordingly they should be the targets for the organization's communications, sales calls and proposals. The marketer needs to know what each member of the DMU wants; and the promotional material which the different parties receive should reflect their own interests and problems.

In many instances, the people who use the organization's products are not the same people as those who make the initial decision to purchase. Sometimes purchasing decisions are taken because organizations are 'locked into' a particular supplier. Often a third party (such as an accountant) within an organization or family can exert strong influence on purchasing decisions. All these people should be taken into account when marketing communications are being planned.

Exercise: At this point, you may care to plan an exercise to be carried out over the next two days or so. Look at two or three commercials on TV during this time and keep any direct mail letters that come to you. For each of these, analyse:

the intended audience for the communication

the message that is being conveyed

the probable promotional objective behind the communication

the probable rationale for using the specific channel of communication selected.

Links with other marketing areas

As we stressed earlier in this chapter, the promotional element of the marketing mix should never be deployed without reference to plans for the other three 'P's.

The benefits associated with the *product* provide the raw material for much promotional activity. The final image projected by promotion will be dictated partly by the product and partly by the promotion itself.

In promotional terms, *price* can be used as an attention-grabber. Another important factor to be considered here is the relationship between price and quality; it is essential, for example, that a premium-priced product should be supported by 'quality' promotion.

The method of *distribution* selected for the product has a strong influence on the type of promotion chosen. A product sold by mail order, for instance, will require a different type of promotion from a product sold in-store. The type of outlet used will also determine the point-of-sale promotional requirements and style. The location, layout and design of store premises offers retailers a promotional tool of great value.

Checklist

In making an assessment of the promotion element of its marketing mix, the organization should:

identify the full range of marketing communications associated with the firm

see promotion in terms of the 'total offer' to the customer

identify the role which promotion should play in the overall marketing effort

go on to set precise and specific promotional objectives

judge its promotional communications in terms of how successfully the message and the medium chosen combine to meet the needs of the target audience

create the 'promotional mix' most appropriate to its target audience's requirements

identify and meet the communication needs likely to be felt by the different members of the DMUs most common in its markets.

22 Promotional Tools and Techniques

Creating a promotional mix

We saw in the last chapter that, just as an appropriate marketing mix has to be devised for the marketing effort overall, so an appropriate promotional mix has to be created for the organization's communications with its markets. Since the range of promotional tools and techniques available in developed economies is vast in scope, marketers must have a clear idea of the armoury at their

```
PRESS - Newspapers
      - Magazines
TELEVISION
RADIO
CINEMA                              ABOVE-THE-LINE
OUTDOOR - Transport
        - Posters & billboards

EXHIBITIONS
SPONSORSHIPS

DIRECT MAIL
BROCHURES & LEAFLETS
POINT-OF-SALE MATERIAL              BELOW-THE-LINE
COMPANY LOGO, LETTERHEAD ETC.
PERSONAL SELLING
```

Figure 22.1. Promotional tools and techniques

disposal before they can devise an integrated and balanced mix of promotional methods. A general description of the promotional tools and techniques available is given in Figure 22.1. In this diagram, the methods have been categorized according to whether they are *above-* or *below-the-line* techniques. Though this distinction may not immediately appear to shed light on a complicated area, it has offered many marketers a perspective which in practice has proved invaluable. In essence, the distinction offers a convenient way for marketers to assess and clarify the purpose and balance of a promotional mix.

As a general rule, above-the-line promotion refers to paid-for space and time, whereas below-the-line promotion involves activities in which space and time are not paid for. Obviously, there are areas of overlap. As Figure 22.1 shows, for example, exhibition space is paid for; however, the promotional activities carried out in this space are not included in the price – they are created separately by the individual exhibitors.

The marketer can also use a 'push–pull' concept to differentiate between above- and below-the-line activities. Generally, below-the-line activities (like personal selling) will be concerned with pushing the product towards the customer; whereas above-the-line activities (like press advertising) will be concerned with pulling the customers towards the product at the point of sale.

Above-the-line techniques

What is advertising good for?

Media advertising is that aspect of promotion with which we, as consumers, are most familiar. But what does it look like from the marketer's point of view? Basically, it involves buying space in one or more of the five traditional media – the press, television, radio, cinema and outdoor/transport media (such as posters) – in order to ensure that:

> **the right information** (benefits of the organization's products/services)
> **from the right people** (the organization)
> **goes to the right people** (the target market)
> **at the right time** (the most appropriate for the product/ service)

in the right manner (the right magazines, journals, etc.)

at the right cost (must be cost effective. How many prod-
ucts/services will have to be sold to meet the advertising
bill?)

Effective advertising requires *precise objectives*. The marketer
should therefore give careful thought to what he or she wants to
achieve through particular advertising campaigns. Advertising can
be used for many different purposes, including:

introducing products/services/businesses to people (that
is, making them aware)

educating people

reminding people

informing people

reinforcing a buying decision

pleasing stockists/intermediaries

building loyalty

creating an image.

The particular aim, or objective, behind advertising will influence
the development and placing of an advertisement in terms of:

the media used

the design of the advertisement

the advertising copy

the typeface of the advertisement

the size of the advertisement

the frequency with which the advertisement appears and
is changed.

Part of setting objectives, that is also a task in its own right, is the
identification of those who are to be the target for advertising. In
other words, what are the target markets? After this broad identification has been made, the marketer should go on to build up a *profile*

of the people making up each target market. (Target markets, you will remember, were the subject of some discussion in Chapter 5.)

This step is a crucial one. Successful communication, after all, depends on the audience being both attracted to the form of the message and interested in the message itself. The marketer must therefore find out just who he or she is talking to in order to tailor the message accordingly. Part of the audience profile should include information on reading, viewing and listening habits and preferences; these factors will influence both the selection of media and the design of the advertisement.

Selecting the media

Given the very wide range of media in the UK, selection of the most appropriate channel (or channels) of communication is a complex task. Many marketers in fact consider it worth while to enlist specialist help in deciding how and where to spend the often considerable sums of money involved. The most appropriate medium is that which will most efficiently provide the marketer with access to his or her target audience in a cost-effective manner. Decisions have to be made on two levels:

1. Which type of communication channel is most likely to convey the right message to the right people (that is, will television or press advertising, say, be more likely to be effective)?

2. Within that branch of the media, which particular vehicle of communication will be most appropriate (that is, which national newspaper, say, will be most popular among the market segment chosen)?

Exercise: Think of an advertisement which you saw recently in your favourite newspaper. Why did the advertiser decide to use press advertising, do you think? And what might have been the reasons for selecting that particular newspaper?

Let us now take a somewhat closer look at the principal advertising media, along with some of the advantages and disadvantages associated with each kind.

Newspapers: The first choice that the advertiser has to make in this area is between *national* and *local* newspapers.

National newspapers have the advantage that they reach vast numbers of people. However, this same fact can also be seen as a disadvantage in the sense that this huge readership varies enormously in life-style, spending power, and so on. In other words, much of the readership is likely to be not interested in a significant proportion of the products or services being advertised. Since advertising space in national papers is extremely expensive, this means that the advertiser may well be 'losing' a considerable amount of his or her investment.

The topicality of national newspapers can also be seen to carry a double edge from the advertiser's point of view. On the one hand, topicality means that newspapers have immediacy and reader interest; on the other hand, however, it means that the publication has a short life-span.

Local newspapers share some of the characteristics of national newspapers – notably a large but undifferentiated audience. However, advertising costs are much lower and the advertiser can be sure of attracting local customers in a geographically compact area.

Consumer magazines: Thousands of consumer magazines appeal to different interest groups in the UK and so offer access to a rather more 'targeted' audience. Whether the advertiser is interested in young mothers, fishermen or photographers, he or she can find the relevant publications conveniently listed in BRAD (British Rate and Data), along with newspapers and other printed media.

The advantages of this medium for the advertiser are that:

> they have a large circulation
>
> copies tend to be passed from person to person
>
> they offer colour printing
>
> they have a relatively long life.

The disadvantages are that:

> advertising is very expensive
>
> long production cycles mean that the copy for the advertising cannot have a topical content
>
> the magazines are swamped by expensive advertising from large companies.

Specialist trade journals: Publications like *The Grocer* offer an identifiable readership which can almost be guaranteed to take an interest in products and services relevant to the particular occupation or industry involved. However, advertising in such journals is often highly competitive and may 'swamp' the reader.

Directories: Directories differ from other media in that they attract customers who are actively looking for specific information on suppliers of various products and services.

Advertisers pay for an entry in such publications in the hope that they will be the supplier eventually chosen. The advantages of this medium are that:

> advertising is relatively cheap
>
> the promotional message has a long life
>
> new customers are constantly being attracted.

The disadvantages are that:

> the promotional message is restricted in size and content
>
> the medium is not eye-catching
>
> slow production cycles mean that publications of this type tend to lack immediacy.

Television: Television has many advantages over printed communications – principally movement and sound. The medium occupies such a prominent place in society that it is often discussed without being specifically mentioned; for example, we have all been party to conversations like, 'Did you see such-and-such last night?'

The automatic understanding is that the 'Did you see . . .?' refers to television; and sometimes the 'Did you see . . .?' refers to advertisements as well as to programmes. Television is a powerful medium; and now that it is possible to schedule a television advertisement for a particular target audience, it is useful for both national advertising and local or regional advertising.

However, for many businesses, television is probably not worth considering because of:

> the high cost of production of an advertisement
>
> the large number of advertisements that need to be placed (in television advertising, *repetition* of the advertising message is one of the keys to success)
>
> the lack of selectivity in the audience it reaches
>
> the short and uncomplicated nature of the promotional message.

Radio: Commercial radio stations offer advertisers localized audiences which have recently shown signs of considerable growth. A careful segmentation of messages can ensure that very different types of audience are reached. Advertising during morning and evening 'drive times', for example, will catch a business and professional audience; while morning advertising will tend to reach housewives. As with television, the main disadvantages of this medium are that the promotional message is a very short one – as is the life of that message. An additional disadvantage is that the product is unseen.

Cinema: Over the last few years this medium has shown declining revenue as a result of falling audiences. However, the advertiser should by no means dismiss it out of hand – particularly if he or she wishes to communicate with an audience of young people.

Advertising messages come across in an effective way, with full use of colour, movement and sound; the cost of using this medium is relatively low; and the advertiser reaches a captive audience which has no distractions.

Outdoor/transport media: The vehicles of communication under this heading include posters, tube trains, buses, taxis and even parking meters.

Poster advertising is relatively inexpensive, but an effective campaign involves the use of many posters in a wide area. Generally speaking, poster advertising is best used to support a television and press campaign, reinforcing a message already communicated in greater detail. The amount of information carried by this medium has to be limited since there is a very short exposure time (that is, car drivers will not see the message for long). On the other hand, the 'life' of the message – in terms of the *number* of exposures – is relatively long compared to other media.

Where the message is displayed on the *outside* of a vehicle, *transport advertising* shows some of the characteristics of poster advertising. In particular, the promotional message must be bold and brief. Where messages are displayed *inside* the vehicle, more detail can be given since the audience is a captive one.

Exercise: Now take a moment to think of three products or services which are familiar to you in either a personal or a business context. Imagine that you have been asked to plan an advertising campaign for each of them. For each product, decide:

    (a) what advertising goals are appropriate

    (b) what is the target audience for your message

    (c) what persuasive message you want to communicate

    (d) which medium is (or media are) most appropriate for your purposes.

Below-the-line techniques

Direct mail

Used properly, direct mail is probably the single most cost-effective method of promotion available to the small business. Large businesses too are making increasing use of direct mail to reach particular market segments; think, for example, of the selection of promotional letters and leaflets which the high street banks enclose with customers' monthly statements.

Exercise: What would you suggest are the main reasons for the popularity of direct mail as a method of promotion?

Compare your suggestions with the following. The main advantages of direct mail are that:

> organizations can use their existing lists of customers as an inexpensive basis for promotion
>
> if necessary, they can also 'buy in' lists of potential customers offering the required market profile
>
> the method allows a high degree of 'targeting' of the audience for the promotion.

Setting objectives: As with all methods of communication, direct mail should be given a clear role within the organization's overall marketing and promotional strategies. This involves setting objectives which are specific and measurable.

Direct mail is likely to be used as an 'opener' – that is, as a first step in the selling process. In this case, the aim of the mail shot is to predispose the recipient to a follow-up telephone call and/or personal visit.

Other uses of direct mail are:

> for direct selling
>
> to generate sales leads
>
> to launch new products/services
>
> to keep existing customers informed and 'happy'.

Mailing lists: A mail-out will only be as good as the list of names and addresses to which it goes. No matter how good the product, how appealing the offer, how creative the material, if the message does not reach the right people, it will all be a waste of money.

There are two requirements for reaching the right people:

(a) *targeting*. It is essential to identify in as much detail as possible the type of people the marketer wishes to contact.

(b) *accurate records.* All too often, mail goes to the wrong people or is incorrectly addressed. Changes in personnel and addresses should be recorded faithfully so that the mailing lists are kept up to date and free of errors.

The direct mail package: The single most important element in most mail-out packages is the letter. Often the letter is supported by material such as leaflets and brochures. But this need not be so. Frequently a letter on its own, well written and with a strong message, is all that is required to obtain a response.

Letters have two distinct advantages over other forms of written communication:

(a) they can be adapted and re-edited at will to take account of changing circumstances;

(b) they can be personalized and the message they contain can be tailored to suit the circumstances of the addressees.

Exercise: Think of a promotional letter which you have received recently. Suggest some reasons why the sender chose to use the medium of direct mail and analyse the success or failure of the persuasive communication as far as you are concerned.

Sales promotions

Sales promotions are made up of the '2p off', '10 per cent discount', 'two for the price of one', 'win a luxury holiday for two' type of short-term promotional offer. Today, about twice as much money is spent on this method of promotion as on media advertising.

Sales promotions are generally aimed at evening out demand fluctuations by boosting short-term sales, rather than at building long-term sales growth. This means that sales promotions are very much a tactical, rather than a strategic, promotional tool. Furthermore, many of the techniques involved are only suited to the promotion of big brands to a mass consumer market.

There are three main target audiences for sales promotions:

consumers

the organization's own sales force or sales agents

the organization's dealers (that is, its wholesalers, distributors or retailers).

The main sales promotion techniques in common use in consumer markets are as follows:

Price cutting: Price cutting has been described as 'a method of slitting your competitor's throat so that you bleed to death yourself'. It is perhaps the most easily recognized – and most abused – sales promotional technique available. The crucial area of decision lies in calculating by how much to lower the price: too little and the demand may not be there; too much, and the organization is giving away its surplus.

Money-off coupons: Coupons in newspaper advertisements, leaflets and show catalogues encourage people to pay more attention to the advertising copy. It has been found that the effectiveness of such coupons as promotional devices depends on their representing an offer of around 15 per cent off the normal price.

Competitions: These can range from putting items in order of importance, to quizzes, to 'Spot the differences' and slogan writing. Usually, an attempt is made to draw a link between the product and the prize, however tenuous this link may be (for example, a Belgian chocolate manufacturer may offer a trip to Brussels). Normally, proof of purchase of the product in question is required for entry to the competition.

Container premiums: These are popular in the gift trade where, for example, Stilton may be sold in 12-oz pottery jars or pewter tankards at a premium price.

Self-liquidators.   This term does not refer to products which self-destruct . . . Self-liquidators are in fact special offers available only to purchasers of a particular product. For example, a manufacturer of sea salt might offer customers the opportunity to buy at a reduced price old-fashioned pottery salt jars.

Multi-pack: This is the 'buy two, get one free' type of offer. A variation on this is where two different but complementary products are sold together, such as shampoo with hair conditioner.

Business gifts: The field is vast: calendars, diaries, telephone pads, pen sets, key rings, paper openers, wall clocks, maps — anything that will take the organization's name and is likely to be kept as a reminder.

Using sales promotions: Some examples of the ways in which sales promotion techniques may be used in particular circumstances are as follows:

(a) *Launching a new/untried product.* The organization may sell samples, offer free trials, guarantee buy-back, introduce sale or return, give the option of delayed payment (a post-dated banker's order is a popular method with magazines).

(b) *Launching a new product which is slightly better than the old one.* For the launch only, the organization may try discounts for bulk orders (buy twelve, get one free), coupons, either on the packet or cut out of a newspaper or handbill ('bring this with you and we'll knock 50p off each item').

(c) *Countering a seasonal demand for a product with year-round production.* The organization may try discounts in the off-season to encourage early purchase, delayed invoicing or giving longer credit. Backed up by a good forward contract, the manufacturer can often approach his suppliers or sub-contractors and negotiate more favourable terms.

Trade fairs and exhibitions

Exhibiting at a trade show is an expensive exercise in terms of both time and money. Unless carefully thought through and handled properly, it can also be a total waste of these scarce resources. Used sensibly, though, trade shows can be a valuable element of the promotional mix by providing:

a testing ground for new products

the opportunity to generate new contacts

the chance to meet up with existing customers.

Exhibitions fall broadly into two distinct categories: trade-only shows, where the visitors are all commercial buyers, and consumer shows for the general public. Some consumer shows often have the first day reserved for trade visitors only. The marketer will obviously have to bear such distinctions in mind when deciding which show to attend.

Setting objectives: As with all promotional activity, there must be clear objectives attached to being an exhibitor. Marketers should ask themselves:

what precisely they hope to achieve by being an exhibitor

whether being an exhibitor is the only way or the most cost-effective way of achieving this objective.

If they are unsure of the answer to either of these questions, they should go back to base and look again at their overall marketing and promotional objectives and strategies.

Exhibitions can be very tempting, so marketers should be particularly ruthless in examining their motives for attending. General guidelines produced by the Institute of Directors include the following:

an exhibition should not be looked upon as an isolated event

never enter an exhibition – no matter how inexpensive it appears to be – unless it fulfils some clearly defined marketing objective

an exhibition should not be regarded as a once-off opportunity to polish up a tarnished image

prestige is never a sufficient reason for appearing at exhibitions don't base exhibition plans on the theory 'if our competitors are there, we have to be there too'

don't try one exhibition just 'to see how it goes'

don't exhibit at all if you have to do it on the cheap – in money or time. This is *not* to say that all exhibitions are expensive; but be sure that you assign adequate money for the job expected to be done

remember: it's ten times easier to start exhibiting than to stop, once you have an exhibition programme under way.

Public relations

Usually referred to as 'PR', public relations is defined by the Institute of Public Relations as 'the deliberate, planned and sustained effort to establish and maintain mutual understanding between an organization and its public'. In practice, however, all too often public relations can simply mean press relations, with all efforts being directed towards the media at the expense of other activities such as open days, sponsorship (see page 225) and community work.

In the sense that it is not directly paid for, PR is not a central part of the promotion element of the marketing mix. However, since its goals are closely related to other promotional goals, it will be included in the present discussion.

Setting objectives: As with all aspects of promotional activity, PR should have clear objectives which derive from the overall marketing objectives of the organization. The objectives should define the people whom the marketer wishes to influence and the message which he or she wishes to get across. Unlike media advertising, PR is intended to influence a larger audience than customers or potential customers. The 'public' may well extend to suppliers, educational institutions and the local community.

Furthermore, PR, perhaps more than any other form of promotion, has a long slow-burning fuse, which means that it is essential to plan on a long-term basis. Developing and projecting a 'good' image (which must also be truthful) cannot happen overnight.

Press relations – publicity

It is useful to realize that most media – the press, television and radio – have very small news-gathering staff and yet rely on news to fill their space or air-time. This means they are constantly looking for news and welcome being fed the 'right' stories from the communities they serve.

The 'right' stories are those which are relevant and interesting for the audience. The chances are that, if the marketer has something interesting to say and says it in the right way, the local newspaper or trade magazine will print it.

The marketer needs to assess those items about his or her organization which are genuinely newsworthy and then pass them in a presentable fashion to the relevant journalist or reporter. Every effort should be made to build good relationships with journalists writing for local newspapers and for relevant trade and technical newspapers and journals.

Company logo and image

Every organization expresses its character through its appearance – and that appearance plays an important part in attracting or discouraging customers. (Not incidentally, a clear and attractive graphic identity also helps to inspire pride and confidence in the organization's own members of staff.)

Exercise: Jot down what you think might be the main promotional vehicles in this area.

Compare your notes with the following suggestions:

> letter headings
>
> packaging
>
> labels
>
> design of premises
>
> promotional materials
>
> transport signwriting.

All these vehicles convey a message about the organization and its products and so need to have a 'feel' consistent with the overall message which the marketer is trying to put across through advertising and other methods of promotion.

Point-of-sale material

Many companies do a good job of bringing people to their businesses by advertising and other promotional methods – but then forget to remind them why they came and why they should buy. Point-of-sale materials – in the form of leaflets, brochures, counter cards, posters, and so on – direct customers to the particular product on offer. This kind of promotion works particularly well when it is used to back up the traditional forms of advertising, such as press or television.

Sponsorship

Many businesses are attracted by the idea of sponsorship – that is, by the thought of their name being associated with prestigious sporting or cultural events. However, the shrewd marketer is careful to undertake a careful cost-effective analysis of this promotional activity *before* committing the organization's resources to it. The fact is that sponsorship often seems to promise more than it delivers: the costs soon mount up and the proven returns are not normally high. Sponsorship activities should be as subject as any other promotional activities to the discipline of objective setting and monitoring.

Personal selling

This method of promotion is sufficiently important to merit a chapter to itself – see Chapter 23.

Checklist

In deciding how to achieve his or her communications objectives, the marketer should:

explore the advantages and disadvantages of the different promotional methods available, including:

media advertising
direct mail
sales promotions
trade fairs and exhibitions
public relations
company image
point-of-sale material
sponsorship
personal selling

assess the balance of the organization's promotional mix in terms of above- and below-the-line techniques

ensure that each promotional technique used fulfils a clear purpose within the overall promotional mix.

23 Selling Skills

Moving into action

Selling is perhaps the most active element of promotion – and of marketing itself. It is the activity directly aimed at getting the customer to buy. If the whole marketing job has been done well, selling is made much easier.

Exercise: Take a moment now to remind yourself why this should be the case. In what ways does sound marketing contribute to effective selling?

You will probably have noted down that a sound marketing programme, involving careful attention to the composition of the marketing mix, will have ensured that the organization will be selling products and services that match customer requirements. In the absence of such a background, the salesperson will find him or herself in the position of trying to sell what the organization happens to have produced rather than what the customer wants.

Selling and the planning and organization of selling (usually known as sales management) constitute a very broad area about which much has been written. In this one chapter, therefore, we can touch on only the most important aspects of the activity.

Sales management

The overall task of sales management is to make the most effective use possible of an organization's sales force – an extremely expensive resource. The essential background to this task is a knowledge of exactly what role personal selling is expected to play in the communications mix.

Chapter 22 concentrated on what might be called *impersonal* ways of communicating with an audience; that is, methods of communication which do not depend on face-to-face encounters with potential customers. However, in many situations a face-to-face meeting is essential for preparing the ground for a sale or for securing the final decision to buy.

Exercise: Note down a number of attributes which you would consider necessary for a successful salesperson. Why is each
of these qualities so important in the task of selling?

Compare your suggestions with ours.

1. Successful salespeople will have in-depth *knowledge* both of their own organization (along with its product-lines) and of the customer's organization. In addition, they will have taken the trouble to get to know the organizational buyer as an individual, with his or her likes and dislikes, areas of sensitivity, and so on.

2. Success in selling partly depends on the ability of the sales-person to project an appropriate *personality*. Personal character-istics such as vitality, sincerity and integrity go a long way towards building up a genuine sympathy between the firm and its customer. It is virtually impossible to create a bond of this kind through impersonal methods of communication.

3. Marked powers of *persuasion* single out the effective sales-person. As we have seen, impersonal methods of communication can work well as tools of persuasion. However, where the sales-person can offer a combination of knowledge and attractive personal characteristics, the task of persuasion is made much easier. In addition, the salesperson can tailor his or her persuasive messages to suit the circumstances of the individual customer. For example, the organization may offer a product in a range of popular colours; but it may well take a face-to-face encounter to persuade a customer that a particular colour is most suitable.

4. Successful salespeople will have equally impressive powers of *judgement*. That is, they will be able to weigh up accurately all the relevant factors operating in a selling situation. Through a combination of accurate evaluation and acute sense of timing, they will know exactly how and when to achieve a sale. This final 'push' is something that no impersonal method of communication can provide.

It can be seen from this checklist that, in certain circumstances, personal selling offers several advantages over impersonal methods of communication. A promotional mix which contains no element of personal selling can run the risk of lacking 'bite'.

But how can this dynamic part of the mix be managed effectively?

The sales manager must be able to find answers to such questions as:

> how many salespeople do I need?
>
> what do I want them to do?
>
> where should they be located?
>
> how should they be organized?

To arrive at the answers, a careful and critical analysis must be made of current practice. A typical manufacturing company might offer the following information on its selling side:

Question	*Possible answers*
Why do we have a sales force?	It's customary; our competitors have sales forces
What does it do?	Opens new accounts
	Services existing accounts
	Demonstrates new products
	Takes repeat orders
	Merchandises
	Collects debts
How does it do it?	Personal visits
Who does it?	Salespeople (men or women)
Where do they do it?	At customers' premises
When do they do it?	During normal working hours

Having gained this information, the company may well find it worth while to explore the possibility of using alternative methods of carrying out some of the sales force's activities. Repeat orders, for example, could well be taken over the telephone rather than during a personal visit; while debts could be collected by mail or by a freelance agency.

Setting and measuring standards

The workload of a salesperson is usually composed of three main elements:

> making calls
>
> travelling
>
> clerical work.

Clearly, the sales manager must find some means of (a) setting targets and standards for the sales force, and (b) checking whether these have been achieved.

This process is best done in conjunction with the salesperson, the tasks being set by mutual agreement. The five main tasks commonly set for a salesperson are:

> to achieve his or her personal sales quotas
>
> to sell the fullest possible range and quantity to individual customers
>
> to plan journeys and call frequencies at optimum selling costs
>
> to seek and gain new customers
>
> to make a sales approach of the required quality.

The standards and performance levels set for each of these tasks will obviously depend on the nature of the overall market situation. For example, if considerable growth is forecast for the target market segment, then the salesperson will be expected to achieve a proportionally high number of new customers. More specifically, standards will be influenced and, in some cases, determined by:

the company's product range in relation to that offered by the competition

the buoyancy of the market

the physical concentration of the customer base

customer circumstances and potential.

Once standards have been agreed and set, the sales manager must monitor actual performance against these standards, noting any variance and taking appropriate action to remedy this. This monitoring process is as much a matter of *motivating* as of *controlling* the sales force.

Motivating and remunerating the sales force

Since selling is a lonely and difficult job, field salespeople need training and constructive feedback as well as adequate financial compensation.

All too often, targets and remuneration levels are imposed on salespeople without prior discussion and agreement. This approach tends to militate against the full commitment of individual members of the sales force to achieving the targets set. Sales managers who seek a motivated commitment to agreed targets and compensation schemes rather than a passive acceptance of management's plans are likely to achieve consistently better sales results from their sales force.

Remuneration falls into three broad categories:

salary only

salary plus commission

commission only.

Probably the most common system of remuneration is salary plus commission, the level of salary often determining the value and standing of the job itself. Sometimes taking the form of bonuses, prizes, and so on, commission is designed to stimulate, motivate and reward dynamic and effective salesmanship.

Commission and salary are very important as motivating factors;

but there are many other, often more effective, motivators. The position and standing of the job itself are matters of great concern to most salespeople; such aspects as scope for achievement and initiative and recognition of success also count for a great deal in the building of good morale in the sales force.

Organizing resources and territories

What is a sales territory? How large is it? In one sense, these questions are similar to the classic 'How long is a piece of string?' A sales territory is built according to the requirements of the market and the optimum use of a company's resources.

Just as the organization's overall market is segmented into distinct customer groupings, so these target market segments in turn are divided up into sales territories. Sales territories are formed according to a number of criteria, including:

> geographical location
>
> customer type and density
>
> patterns of product usage.

These criteria are not necessarily mutually exclusive; indeed they often combine to determine a territory, as is shown in Figure 23.1. In this example, a territory could be determined geographically or by customer type; that is, any one territory might be focused on all

Geographical area

	A – South-east	B – Midlands	C – North
Industrial customers			
'Consumer' customers			
Service customers			

Type of customer

Figure 23.1.   Sales territory matrix

customers in the South-east or on industrial customers in the South-east, the Midlands and the North.

Obviously, a company's resources must be matched as closely as possible with the requirements of the market-place. However, the sales manager must also deal with the issue of a fair division of territories among his or her salespeople.

Preparing and planning to sell

Before attempting to sell a product, salespeople must have a clear idea of the customers to whom the selling effort is being directed. They will then be able to tailor their approach to each individual customer, and receive a response from the right people at the right time.

Exercise: Do you remember the distinction made in Chapter 6 between existing and potential customers and between the immediate customer and the end user? What relevance do you think these distinctions might have for the selling activity?

An *existing* customer is someone with whom the organization is already doing business. As such, this customer will need a briefer introduction to the nature of the organization and its product range than will a completely new *potential* customer. However, the existing customer may also be a *potential* customer for other products offered by the organization. Salespeople must make sure that they get to know the customer's overall requirements sufficiently well that they can recognize and take advantage of further sales opportunities.

The *immediate* customer may well have several other people standing behind him or her, so to speak. This is because the immediate customer may well be a member of a DMU (check back to Chapters 6 and 7 if you have forgotten quite what this concept means). In this case, the salesperson will have to find out exactly what information each member of the decision-making unit needs and then go on to provide the information in an acceptable form. For instance, the immediate customer may not be the *end user* of the product being sold. In this case, the customer will have to be satisfied that the product will meet with the approval of this end user. To make a successful sale in these circumstances, therefore, the salesperson must have a clear idea of the needs of the end user as well as those of the immediate customer.

Exercise: Take a moment now to look at Table 23.1. Think of a product or service which you know well. Imagine that you are responsible for selling it and then fill in the boxes to give the most detailed picture you can of the different people involved in the buying decision.

Table 23.1.   *Who decides to buy?*

	Analysing who shares in the decision to buy your products, or use your services
Customer you are dealing with.	
Product or service you are trying to sell.	
People who will have a part in that decision. Any comments.	
Ways in which you should seek to give people information and influence them positively.	

Setting objectives

Each sales call must have clear objectives. Salespeople who do not have a clear reason for their calls are unlikely to bring about a positive 'close' (that is, a satisfactory conclusion) to the call.

The objective need not necessarily be 'to achieve a sale'. In many industries – and especially in capital goods industries – the selling process progresses through a series of stages of investigation and negotiation between customer and seller. Each development call to a particular organization may have a different objective, such as:

> to find out about the business

> to obtain a trial order

> to establish a repeat-order routine

> to find out who are the key people influencing the buying process

> to handle a complaint

> to present a quotation, specification or other documents.

Planning the sales interview

Having set clear objectives, the salesperson must develop a plan for achieving them – and then remember to use it in the interview itself. In the stress of the interview, it is all too easy to forget the intended approach.

A useful sequence to follow in both the planning and conducting of the sales interview is the 'ABC method'. This approach is one of arresting the customer's **A**ttention, presenting the **B**enefits of the product or service in a clear and logical manner, then **C**losing the deal.

While thinking through the relevant benefits of his or her offer, the salesperson should also give some thought to the *objections* that the customer may raise – for example, 'It's too expensive,' or 'That wouldn't work in my business.' Some objections are fundamental ones and, as such, are hard, even impossible, to counter. However, others can be met quite satisfactorily by the salesperson if he or she has taken the time to think out satisfactory answers.

Salespeople should prepare with care any supporting material (like visual aids, brochures or leaflets) that they may need during the interview. They should make sure that the material is relevant, well presented, complete and in good order.

Making the appointment

Making appointments on the telephone with new potential customers is often called 'hard selling'. If customers feel that such tactics are 'hard' on them, then there is perhaps some consolation in the fact that the salesperson also often experiences stress in these situations.

Exercise: Can you suggest some reasons why this approach is 'hard' for the salesperson?

Compare your suggestions with the following:

> the salesperson will usually run up against the 'shields' (like protective secretaries) which surround most senior executives

> the salesperson will have to have carried out adequate preparation for the phone call so that he or she can offer a convincing case for being granted an interview

> the salesperson will have only a short time in which to present his or her case to a possibly hostile listener.

Assuming that the salesperson has been able to make his or her case convincingly, the next step is to take the initiative in suggesting a date and time for the interview. This is usually seen by the customer as a positive move and it helps the salesperson to keep control of his or her daily timetable.

Ready to talk

Thorough preparation of the kind discussed above ensures that the salesperson:

> knows the customer

> knows his or her own products

> is aware of previous dealings with the customer

> has thought through what the customer may want and be interested in

has thought through possible objections that the customer may have, along with ways of countering these.

The sales interview

There is a great deal of literature on the sales interview, much of it describing the different approaches which can be taken. Although there is frequent variation on detailed strategies, all authorities agree that each interview must consist of a process which moves smoothly from a beginning through a middle to an end.

Exercise: Do you remember what was involved in the ABC method mentioned earlier in this chapter? Note down the basic features of the method.

As you might expect, different skills and techniques are required for each element of the process; and a salesperson must be well prepared in each area.

The interview itself can be broken down into four main stages: the opening approach; identifying needs; selling benefits; and negotiating and closing.

The opening approach

The salesperson must get this right. If he or she gets off on the wrong foot, it will be very difficult to retrieve the situation. The approach can often begin with *brief* social niceties, such as comments on business, the customer's family, holidays, and so on. Obviously, the content of this part of the conversation will depend on whether or not the salesperson knows the customer well – and the extent to which the customer invites and enjoys such conversation.

Essentially, the opening approach is concerned with 'breaking the ice' and assessing the potential and receptiveness of the customer. The salesperson must be quick to weigh up all the circumstances of the meeting. If the customer is very busy, then he or she is unlikely to pay full attention to what is being said; if the customer shows little interest, then a 'soft sell' approach may be necessary; if the customer is keen, then a 'straight to the point' approach may be most appropriate.

Identifying needs/asking questions

This stage should be reached at an early point in the interview. The objective here is to assess the customer's needs and wants; and this entails gathering information. Observation will provide some clues, but by far the best way to get information is to ask questions.

Obviously, the nature of these questions will depend on the specific situation at hand. However, there are clear 'do's and 'don't's about the *type* of question to be asked at this stage. The salesperson should ask open-ended, probing, prompting questions – the kind of questions which require an explanation or description in reply. He or she should avoid asking the 'closed' type of questions – that is, those questions which require only 'yes', 'no' or other monosyllabic answers.

Examples of 'open' questions would include:

On business

How is business?

What do you think is causing sales to increase/decline?

What are the most popular lines?

How do you think business will be in the future?

On products

Which products do you use and why do you choose them?

How many do you use and how often?

On quality

What standards do you work to?

How important are quality and reliability to you?

On delivery

What stocks do you carry?

How quickly do you need supplies?

Selling benefits and providing facts

If the salesperson has identified the customer's needs correctly, this part of the interview may be relatively simple. Questions continue to be valuable tools, since the customer's answers may well point up the benefits associated with the product or service being sold. As the customer answers the salesperson's questions, he or she often begins to recognize the benefits that are involved; in short, customers begin to sell the product to themselves.

The following exchange illustrates this point:

CUSTOMER: I want a waterproof watch.

SALESPERSON: When are you going to use the watch?

CUSTOMER: On the beach on holiday, and later on when we go on a canal barge.

SALESPERSON: But you're not going to use it actually in the water?

CUSTOMER: But there might be spray or an accident?

SALESPERSON: Of course, but these watches are protected from incidental contact with water and they are a fraction of the cost of the fully waterproof ones like divers use.

CUSTOMER: Hmm . . . let me see one of them.

Negotiation and close

The salesperson must be able to recognize the moment at which he or she can fruitfully close the interview. The close can take various forms, depending on the objectives which the salesperson has set for the meeting; it may involve asking for an order or, on the other hand, it may simply consist of an agreement to meet again to present a proposal.

Knowing just when to close the interview depends on being able to pick up and interpret the 'buying signals' transmitted by the customer. These signals may be quite clear – as when, for instance, the customer asks about delivery arrangements, quantity discounts, and so on. At times, however, the salesperson will have to rely on close observation and insight in order to detect the drift of the customer's comments. The customer may want to negotiate, for example – in which case he is interested in finding a point of trade-off between himself and the salesperson. The customer may raise some objections to the salesperson's offer at this point; but the well-prepared salesperson will be able to counter these objections with appropriate arguments or concessions.

Considerable skill is essential if the maximum sale possible is to be obtained. The salesperson should probe for as large an order as possible – but should also take care not to antagonize the customer.

Having achieved a sale for a particular product, the salesperson can sometimes explore the possibility of selling complementary products and services. However, this exploration should be undertaken with due care; prolonging an interview against the customer's wishes can do untold damage.

Checklist

In making the most effective use of the personal selling element of its promotional mix, the organization should:

identify the precise role to be played by personal selling within its communications mix

have a clear idea of the attributes necessary for successful salespeople

establish an effective sales management function which will:
set and monitor standards
motivate and remunerate the sales force in the most appropriate way
organize resources and territories
train the sales force to plan and conduct effective sales interviews.

In addition, individual salespeople should:

undertake all necessary preparation for a sales visit

make an appointment and plan the interview

sell benefits

overcome objections

achieve a satisfactory close.

24 The 'Right' Promotion

Building up a promotional campaign

The last three chapters should have made at least one thing clear: no marketer need ever feel that he or she has too little choice of promotional methods. It is highly likely, though, that at one time or another every marketer will feel swamped by the variety of tools available and will have some difficulty in making choices among them.

So, how *can* these choices be made? What *is* the 'right' promotion for any individual product or service? As usual, the easy answer is neither particularly helpful nor particularly practical. The 'right' promotion, marketing theory tells us, is that co-ordinated promotional campaign which best fulfils objectives within the constraint of available resources.

How can this (perfectly correct) statement be broken down into terms that make sense on a practical level? First of all, the marketer must set his or her promotional objectives in the context of the over-all marketing objectives for the product. Secondly, the marketer must aim to establish a promotional mix which achieves these objectives. Thirdly, the marketer must assess in a systematic way whether this mix is (a) achieving the objectives, and (b) achieving the objectives in a cost-effective manner. If it is doing neither of these things, then the mix must be changed.

The marketer faced with this daunting task can take some comfort from the concept of a *promotional campaign*. This refers to a totally integrated programme of promotion in which a series of promotional activities are built round a single idea and designed to achieve some specific objectives. Thus, a promotional campaign can be divided into, say, its advertising, personal selling, sales promotion and direct mail components.

An organization may conduct several different types of promotional campaign at once, depending on the promotional objectives and the resources available. The campaigns may have a local, regional or national focus; and they may be aimed at different target audiences – at consumers, for example, or at wholesalers and sales agents.

As always, the setting of the main objective comes first. This objective, along with the buying motives of the customers, will determine the nature of the promotional message. A railway, for example, may wish to enhance the image of its sleeping car service; and to do this it might appeal to the desire of long-distance business travellers to avoid some of the disadvantages associated with air travel, such as early morning rush and worry about traffic jams at the other end of the journey. In this case, national newspaper and poster advertising campaigns might be considered to be the most appropriate media through which to reach the target market.

However diverse the activities associated with it, a promotional campaign centres on one main idea. This 'theme' – as in British Rail's 'We're getting there' – permeates all promotional efforts and seeks to unify the campaign.

Exercise: Take a moment to think of a 'theme' currently running through the promotional acitivities of a major British company or concern. Note down the different promotional contexts in which you have found this theme expressed. For each promotional method you have identified, analyse how the theme is used to focus the audience's attention on the other promotional messages being presented.

The success of any promotional campaign depends on the effective co-ordination of the different elements involved. Thus, the sales force must ensure that they explain and demonstrate the product benefits communicated in the advertising; while the point-of-sale material must reinforce the image and message being carried by above-the-line promotion (see Figure 22.1 again).

Factors influencing the promotional mix

Decisions on the composition of the promotional mix have to be taken in the light of the following factors.

Resources available

Financial constraints will obviously play a crucial part in determining which promotional methods can be used. For example, although small firms might wish to gain the communication benefits offered by television as a medium, they are unlikely to be able to afford the cost of television advertising. The fact is that firms with a substantial promotional budget are in a much better position to make effective use of above-the-line promotion. Small firms are more likely to rely on personal selling, on sales promotions and on other below-the-line activities.

Nature of the market

As always in marketing, the nature of the particular market and customer groups involved goes a long way to shaping the decisions made by the marketer. The key questions involved here are:

How large is the market in geographical terms? If the market is small and local, then personal selling, possibly combined with the distribution of door-to-door circulars, is likely to be the most effective means of communication. A widely spread market, however, is usually most efficiently tackled by advertising of one kind or another.

How concentrated is the market? If the total number of prospective buyers is relatively small (as is the case, for example, in many capital-goods markets), then personal selling will probably be the main method of promotion. The marketer must also consider the number of different *types* of potential customer involved. If the organization's products are of interest only to publishers of medical books, say, then again personal selling will suggest itself as a major promotional activity. However, if the organization's products are of interest to *all* publishing firms, then advertising in trade magazines and attendance at trade fairs will probably present themselves as much more efficient channels of communication.

What type of customers characterize the market?   Different types of customer expect a different kind of promotional approach. For example, intermediaries, such as wholesalers, may well expect personal visits from members of the sales force; while consumers in a mass market will be more accustomed to assimilating promotional messages through television, press and poster advertising.

Nature of the product

The nature of the product being sold is of considerable significance when the decision is being made on just how to promote it. A mass market consumer product, for example, will usually be mainly supported in promotional terms by a mass advertising campaign, along with point-of-sale displays. This kind of approach fits in with the nature of the product itself; it appeals to many people and needs no special explanation or demonstration.

The manufacturer of specialized X-ray equipment for hospital use, however, can expect to devote most of his promotional effort to personal contact with a number of key hospital staff: doctors, radiographers, engineers, medical physicists, and so on. In this case, the investment made by the customer is a large one; some modifications to the product may need to be made; and high levels of before- and after-sales service are needed to ensure that the deal progresses smoothly.

As the above examples suggest, the chief division in the communications mix is between advertising and personal selling. Some products are more suited to an emphasis on personal selling; in this case, the marketer can be seen as adopting a *push strategy*, where the organization is concentrating its efforts on moving the product through the distribution channel towards the customer. Where the nature of the product leads to an emphasis on advertising as a method of promotion, the organization can be seen as deploying a *pull strategy*. In this case, the consumers are attracted and drawn to the point of sale where the product is available and highly visible.

Stage in the product life-cycle

The basic nature of the product is not the only feature of the product
to influence promotional methods chosen. Important too is the stage
of its life-cycle that the product has reached.

Exercise: Can you remember the main features of the product life-
cycle theory? If not, look back at the relevant sections of
Chapters 12 and 13.

The *introductory* stage of a product's life-cycle is marked by the need
to inform and educate potential customers about the basic nature
of the product type. Personal selling to dealers and attendance at
exhibitions and shows are usually the preferred methods of promotion at this stage. Any advertising is of an informative nature,
giving details of performance, use and effectiveness.

At the *growth* stage of the product, customer awareness has
increased and brand differentiation has begun to make itself felt.
Advertising now often assumes a greater importance in the
promotional mix, emphasizing the differences between the various
competing products.

The *maturity-saturation* stage is marked by the intensification of
competition and a levelling-off in sales. Advertising is now used to
persuade rather than inform. The large sums spent on advertising
contribute to declining profits; however, these sums are often offset
by the economies of scale achieved through maintaining high sales.

At the *sales-decline* stage, all promotional efforts need to be
pruned substantially, except where the specific goal is to 'rejuvenate'
the product. Often, advertising can be 'concentrated' on the hard
core of loyal repeat purchasers or essential users rather than the
mass market. It is highly unlikely that any new customers will be
captured unless a rejuvenation strategy is introduced.

Determining the 'right' mix

After considering the effects of the different factors discussed above, the marketer can move fairly rapidly to the point of decision in the matter of the promotional mix. The following guidelines can help to focus the decision-making process in this area.

Personal selling will predominate the mix when:

    adequate resources are not available for an advertising campaign

    the market is of a concentrated nature

    the product needs careful explanation and support

    the product has a high unit value

    the product has to be tailored to the customer's needs.

Personal selling may be undertaken either through the company's own representatives and agents or through representatives attached to intermediaries.

Advertising will be emphasized in the mix when:

    the market for the product is widespread

    the marketer wishes to communicate to many people quickly

    high market share is desirable.

Point-of-sale promotion will play a prominent part when:

    the product has qualities which can be judged easily at the point of purchase

    the product is a very standardized item

    the product is of a type which is subject to 'impulse buying'

    the name of the retailer is more familiar to potential customers than that of the manufacturer.

In the main, the promotional mix will consist of a combination of above-the-line (advertising) and below-the-line (personal selling and point-of-sale) activities. The particular circumstances surrounding the product and its market will dictate the *emphasis* given to the various promotional tools.

Exercise: Think of a product which you know well. Which method predominates in the promotional mix associated with this product? Suggest some reasons as to why this method was selected to play the major role in promotion. Do you agree with the decision to allocate resources in this way? Give reasons for or against your stance on this.

Setting promotional expenditure budgets

The type of expenditure here will vary according to company and market requirements. If a company needs to emphasize personal selling, for example, then clearly manpower and facilities will require considerable expenditure. If, on the other hand, advertising is the main method of communication deployed, then substantial resources will have to be channelled into advertisement design and creation; media space and time; and promotional material, such as posters, leaflets, sales letters, brochures, and so on.

How much to spend on advertising?

A business may organize its own advertising campaign or it may delegate this activity to advertising agents. In either case, decisions have to be made regarding:
1. how much money is to be spent on advertising?
2. how should this amount vary from year to year to match fluctuations in market conditions?

As yet there are no hard and fast rules to follow in this area. Whether the amount involved is £1,000 or £1,000,000, organizations have to do the best they can against a background of conflicting expert opinion.

The following practical methods of assessing the 'right' expenditure level are in common use – though, as we shall see, all are open to criticism.

1. 'Percentage of sales' methods

According to these methods, advertising appropriation should be assessed as a percentage of sales turnover. Expressed either as a fixed figure or as a fluctuating figure depending on other variables, the percentage can be applied to past, current or estimated future turnover.

The main criticism of this method is directed at its use of past or current turnover as the basis for the advertising budget. Since the purpose of advertising is to increase demand beyond the levels it would otherwise reach, this measuring stick would appear to have little logical foundation. Advertising, after all, should be presumed to be the *cause* of sales.

A further argument against this method is that the use of *future* sales as a measuring stick is also unsound. Future sales, after all, will be the cumulative result of many different factors in addition to advertising – for example, the level of national income, the effects of past advertising, and the effects of competitors' current advertising.

However, despite its obvious disadvantages, this method of assessing the 'right' level of advertising expenditure remains popular. The reasons probably include:

> the lack of a more logical method of measurement

> the *illusion of control* obtained by relating the intangible element of expense in a systematic way to the very tangible element of revenue

> the fact that if most competitors in an industry use this method and apply approximately the same percentage, then the outlay on advertising will approximate to each competitor's share of the market. This has a restraining effect on advertising warfare.

2. The 'all you can afford' method

It can be argued that a profitable firm can afford to spend on advertising either:

    (a) profits over and above a minimum required return
       or
    (b) all profits
       or
    (c) all profits + a proportion of cash reserves
       or even
    (d) all profits + cash reserves + borrowed funds.

While at first sight this method appears to have little to recommend it, it must be said that the effects of advertising outlays on profit and liquidity are important considerations in setting the upper limits of advertising expenditure.

Normally the delay between expenditure on advertising and the actual result in terms of sales is considerable; and to ignore the availability of short-term cash and credit limits may cause financial embarrassment.

Looked at in this light, it is the resources of the company that set a real limit on expenditure.

Used uncritically, this method is unsatisfactory since there is no valid relationship between liquidity and advertising opportunities. That is, liquidity *is* a practical constraint for an organization – but is not an indicator of the viability of future advertising.

3. The 'objective and task' method

Here the budget is the amount estimated to be required to achieve a certain objective. This objective might be a 10 per cent increase in sales beyond what they would be without advertising; or it could consist of establishing a brand name as a household word.

This method begs the question: just how *do* you measure the value of an objective and determine the cost of achieving it?

4. The 'as much as your competitor' method

In this method, an attempt is made to base the organization's outlay in some systematic way on that of its competitors. In other words, outlay will approximate to share of the market.

The difficult part here lies in getting to know one's competitors' exact circumstances. For example, they may be attempting to expand and capture some of your share and hence be spending particularly heavily on advertising.

Advocates of this method claim that (a) it safeguards against advertising warfare, and (b) the total advertising expenditure of an industry represents the combined wisdom of the industry. The second claim, it should be noted, presupposes that the organization's competitors know what they are doing – not an assumption that everyone would be happy about.

In addition, the method may be criticized on the grounds that competitors' *future* rather than *past* expenditure should constitute the measuring stick. But, normally, this figure cannot be determined with enough speed or accuracy to be much help to the organization planning its advertising budget.

Clearly none of the appropriation methods discussed above is totally satisfactory in itself. This being the case, marketers often combine elements of the different methods to find the appropriation levels most sensible for them. Having accepted that there is a variety of influences on advertising appropriation – past sales, company objectives and resources, competitive activities, and so on – they proceed to take all these into account when deciding how much to spend.

Exercise: How does your own organization, or an organization well known to you, judge how much to spend on advertising? What are the advantages of the method it uses and what are the disadvantages?

Evaluating promotion

It makes sense to try to assess whether or not a promotional campaign is being, or has been, effective. There are two quite separate aspects to this process of evaluation:

the *communications* effect: does the promotional activity succeed in conveying the desired message?

the *sales* effect: what impact has the promotional activity had on sales?

It is extremely difficult to measure either of these effects with any real degree of accuracy. However, the prior setting of clear objectives (as discussed in Chapter 22) does help the marketer to judge how successful the promotional effort has been on these two different dimensions.

Marketing research too can give good feedback on promotional effectiveness. If used properly, some of the techniques discussed in Chapter 9, such as consumer surveys on perceptions and attitudes and observation studies on purchasing behaviour, can help in the evaluation of promotional campaigns. Such results, of course, form only part of the picture. A fuller picture will emerge when these results are combined with other evaluations, such as sales figures and assessment of competitor activities.

Many marketers, though, would still nod their heads in agreement with one practitioner's comment: 'I know that half my promotion is ineffective – the trouble is, I don't know which half.'

In the context of evaluation, however, it is vital to remember that promotion is an investment rather than an on-cost, so its returns are spaced over time.

Checklist

In determining the promotional mix most appropriate for particular products, the organization should:

plan promotional activities in terms of an integrated campaign take the following factors into account when deciding which promotional methods to use:

  financial resources available
  nature of the market
  nature of the product
  stage in the product life-cycle

choose between the following methods of assessing the 'right' expenditure methods:

  the 'percentage of sales' methods
  the 'all you can afford' method
  the 'objective and task' method
  the 'as much as your competitors' method

attempt to assess how successful the campaign has been in terms of both *communications* effects and *sales* effects.

4 Marketing Strategies and Planning

25 The Process of Strategy Planning

Why bother with planning?

Marketing planning would not be necessary if the business environment could be guaranteed to remain the same as it is today and if there were no likelihood of the organization itself undergoing any internal changes.

However, in today's climate, how many organizations can expect to remain static in an unchanging business world? (If you have answered 'none', then you are not far off the mark.)

For most companies today, market expectations are changing so fast that it is hard to know what customers will expect tomorrow – let alone what to anticipate from the more aggressive competitors. And all of this has taken place in a business environment that is also experiencing dramatic change. In recent years, organizations have operated in a period of foreign exchange fluctuations, volatile interest rates, changes in government regulations, increases in imports and indirect competition and changes in social habits.

To deal with the changes and organize themselves for the future, organizations need to make the best use of their resources. Whatever decisions they make, a consistent strategic approach is most likely to achieve their goals. And for this they need a good marketing plan.

A successful planned approach to marketing should achieve the following benefits:

> improvement in profit targets and investment return
>
> focus on the company's selected markets
>
> efficient use of the company's scarce resources
>
> use of company and product strengths working together
>
> development of new products and markets for the future
>
> a proactive approach to change (that is, *anticipating* change rather than just reacting to it when it happens)
>
> additional business concentrated in areas of competitive strength.

But these benefits do not come easily. Marketing planning is probably the most difficult and mind-stretching aspect of a marketing manager's job – if, that is, it is done properly.

What is planning about?

So, what is planning about? It is about looking to the future and attempting to anticipate events and trends; it is about identifying and exploiting key market opportunities which may arise; and it is about thinking through how the company can make the most of these opportunities.

Planning can be carried out over a range of time scales. Short-range planning can cover anything from three months to a year; medium-range planning may involve a one- to three-year time horizon; while long-range planning can stretch from three years onwards. These figures are merely rough guidelines. Planning horizons depend very much on the nature of the industry involved. In the pop record industry, for example, the 'short term' may be as immediate as days or weeks; while in the aerospace industry, long-range planning and development can refer to a twenty-year period of time.

The decisions involved in planning are of a different order from those involved in day-to-day marketing operations. Day-to-day marketing decisions commonly:

> require immediate action
>
> give instant results
>
> keep customers happy
>
> direct/guide subordinates
>
> solve immediate crises.

Most operational-type decisions focus on the 'now' situation; that is, they are concerned with the immediate environment of business activity. Marketing planning, on the other hand, consists of decisions which involve careful thought about:

> the future
>
> forecasting/estimating
>
> protecting ideas
>
> working to a clear course of action
>
> objectives which can be met
>
> strategies that can be followed.

Most planning decisions focus on the 'future' situation; that is, they are concerned primarily with issues which are not of immediate or short-term concern, but instead will become important in the long term.

In practice, how do marketing managers achieve a balance between planning for the future and living in the present? You may not be surprised to learn that in fact many never do find a suitable balance. Immediate problems often seem so pressing that future problems are pushed away for 'rainy day' consideration. In addition, many managers much prefer to make 'here and now' decisions rather than long-term decisions for the simple reason that these decisions are more immediately gratifying. The results of these decisions can easily be seen and, generally speaking, the result 'closes' the problem – that is, the decision is seen to have worked. Obviously, the same cannot be said of most long-term decisions.

To sum up then, marketing planning is essential to any organization's success in the market-place. It is, however, a process commonly associated with considerable difficulty, complexity and uncertainty.

Exercise: Do you have any experience of making marketing decisions for the future? If so, what did you find most difficult in this task? If not, what difficulties have you found in making personal plans for the future?

A systematic approach to planning

Fortunately, recent years have seen the development of a systematic approach to marketing strategy planning, an approach which reduces some of the difficulties for management and some of the uncertainty of the planning itself. Usually called the *marketing planning process*, this approach is based on a series of logical steps

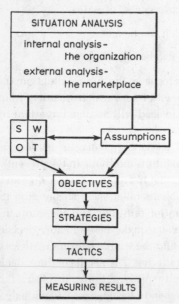

Figure 25.1.   The marketing planning process

and decision stages which are in turn based on the sound principles of marketing described in earlier chapters. Figure 25.1 illustrates the scope of the marketing planning process.

Situation analysis

The starting point for the planning process is familiar to you since it was introduced in Chapter 8. The 'situation analysis', you may remember, consists of examining evidence both internal and external to the organization in order to arrive at an objective assessment of the organization's current position *vis-à-vis* the markets it serves.

You may find a brief summary helpful. The *internal* part of the analysis involves assessing *all* aspects of the organization's activities, not just the marketing function itself. Thus, consideration should be given to the company's overall resources – human, financial and physical (plant and equipment). In addition, assessment should be made of the organization's present marketing policies. How effective are they? How relevant are they? Do they achieve the desired goals? Each of the four 'P's should also be subjected to searching analysis. For example, is there a balanced product range? What new product ideas are in the pipeline?

The *external* part of the analysis consists of an examination of the market-place. This means analysing all the relevant environmental factors – such as economic trends or technological innovations – as well as customers and competitors. Although these factors are outside the control of the organization, the more that is known about them the less uncertain is the market-place and the more stable the foundations of the marketing plan.

If the situation analysis seems an impossibly abstract task, then you may find it interesting to hear what one practitioner has to say about it. An engineer by training, Seamus Connolly developed an innovative product, Fastank, a unique and soundly engineered container: lightweight, easily assembled and suitable for storing liquids and granular materials. In the passage which follows he describes here how his newly formed company, Fast Engineering Ltd, set about making an initial exploration of market conditions.

I started with published material and cut out clippings from the local news-papers and from engineering magazines. I kept them for future reference and any relevant articles from books I photocopied. All these pieces were just dumped in a box in the corner but proved very worth while when I did get down to doing some serious structuring of the market!

> It actually identified where the market need lay

> It gave me some idea of the amount of money that was being spent in this particular area

> It indicated the needs of relief organizations that were crying out for assistance in water

> It introduced me to the 'Decade of Water and Sanitation' and the people who were promoting it.

Very shortly I was able to pick out the key people interested in water, and associated areas. I was also able to examine the competition, look at their advertisements, look at their pricing, which magazines they advertised in, etc. I wrote to these companies as a potential customer – as if I was going to buy a tank – and they were most forthcoming with details, materials samples and prices, which I think would have been very difficult to get otherwise. So I got in under the guise of a customer as opposed to a competitor, which gave me a great insight. I was able to examine their brochures and choose which would be most suitable for my product, pick out their benefits, their unique selling points and see how they sold their products. And I was able to refine all this information down.

All this is simply good sense, you may think, and a long way away from the type of formal analysis described above. However, a moment's reflection would show that Seamus Connolly *did* in fact follow the various steps involved in a situation analysis – although he called them by different names. He considered all the relevant external factors in the context of his internal capabilities. He was then able to 'structure' the data he had acquired into meaningful information about the nature and requirements of the market and an analysis of how best to exploit the opportunities. The concept of the situation analysis may appear to be impossibly abstract; but, in practice, it is firmly based on good sense.

It is also important to remember that Seamus Connolly's common-sense approach evolved over a period of time. It took him time to gather the data; time to accumulate it into meaningful information; time to develop and refine his product and marketing. There was nothing instant or 'now' about this process; instead, it involved the past, present and, particularly, the future. It was, in fact, a typical marketing planning cycle.

SWOT

Once completed, the information generated by the situation analysis needs to be organized in a way that makes it usable. SWOT analysis provides the framework for this.

As explained in Chapter 8, SWOT analysis involves looking at all the information collected and analysing the implications of all the facts, figures, opinions and conjectures under the four headings: organization **S**trengths; organization **W**eaknesses; market **O**pportunities and market **T**hreats. The resulting summary is both cornerstone and starting point for most marketing plans.

Making assumptions

It is never possible to know for certain what the future will bring, however good our information on the present and feel for the future. Nevertheless, an essential ingredient of marketing planning is the construction of a picture of the future against which marketing strategies can be developed. Hence there is a need to make *assumptions* about what will and will not happen.

Assumptions may be made about any aspect of the market-place – market trends, competitors' activities, and so on. Examples might include statements like, 'No further competitors will enter the market in the next three years,' or 'Levels of imported goods will increase above current levels by more than 3 per cent per annum.'

It is important to rank assumptions in order of importance and to assess the degree of confidence with which they are made. This can be done by asking the following questions about each assumption in turn:

1. How large an impact does this assumption have on the conclusions I am drawing?
2. How accurate does this assumption need to be to alter the conclusions?

3. What level of certainty can I place on the correctness of my assumption?

Some assumptions will emerge as incidental to the planning process; others will become critical. Constant monitoring of the critical assumptions is vital. This is because plans may well need to be redrawn if a critical assumption proves false.

Part of the value of a formal marketing process lies in the pressure it exerts on managers to control their intuitive instincts. It is often in making assumptions that managers give most freedom to their subjective judgements. The process of making their assumptions explicit and providing a rationale for these assumptions helps many managers make more informed and objective judgements.

Setting marketing objectives

Marketing objectives are not the only objectives essential to good and sound business performance. However, since marketing activity can be diffuse and, at times, intangible and difficult to control, most managers feel the need to devote particularly careful consideration to formulating realistic marketing objectives.

Using the information arising from the situation analysis, as well as the results of the SWOT analysis and list of assumptions, management can set short-, medium and long-term objectives which will, in the words of one manager, 'get us where we want to go'. It is important that the objectives should be precise and measurable: for example, one objective might be 'to enter market A with product B and achieve a 5 per cent market share within a year'. The objectives will set the organization on a marketing course of action which will demand considerable levels of commitment and determination. The objectives themselves should therefore be understood by all relevant managers within the organization and, ideally, be fully accepted by them.

Managers must steel themselves against the temptation to make panic changes. Above all else, what is needed is *confidence* in the objectives set. This confidence should be based on knowledge that the planning process to date has been carried out thoroughly and objectively, and that everything has been done to determine the most appropriate objectives.

Marketing objectives founded on the uncertainty of intuition alone will quickly seem inappropriate when adverse market forces begin to make themselves felt. Methodically set marketing objectives may also have to be revised in the light of dramatically changing market circumstances. But revision in this case will not be a sudden panic measure; the objectives will be revised only after the same methodical examination of circumstances that established them in the first place.

Developing marketing strategies and plans

If marketing objectives are the 'where we want to go' of marketing, then strategies and tactics provide the 'how we're going to get there' element.

Strategies should establish in broad terms the courses of action that will be followed in order to achieve the marketing objectives. (Americans call this part of the process 'the game plan'.) The nature and character of the objectives should be reflected in the type of strategies chosen. For example, if the marketing objective is to establish a top-quality image over a given period of time, then the strategies will constantly feature 'quality' and all the surrounding attributes of quality, such as reliability, sophistication, attention to detail, customer service, and so on.

In addition, sound marketing strategies will utilize the results of the SWOT analysis by building on strengths and matching these with market opportunities, tackling weaknesses, drawing out hidden strengths and avoiding areas of threat.

Tactics involve greater attention to detail. They are the short-term decisions and activities which push forward the course of action laid down by the strategies. Tactics, like strategies, cover all the elements of the marketing mix – but for a more limited period and in greater detail.

Where the marketing objectives provide the overall direction for an organization's activity, the marketing strategies and tactics provide the broad schedule and detailed itinerary for achieving the objectives.

You may find the analogy of a railway journey useful in sorting out in your mind the differences between objectives, strategies and tactics. The objective is the railway terminus; the strategies are the rails by which we reach the station; and the tactics are the different elements of the journey along the rails. These might include the speed of the journey, the stops at intermediate stations, and the service provided for us along the way.

Of course, organizations do not usually have a single marketing objective, one strategy and one set of tactics. More often there are several strings to the marketing bow. This makes it even more essential that all aspects of marketing activity are knitted together into an integrated whole and that tactics are translated into co-ordinated task schedules. Marketing planning helps achieve integration and provides the background discipline necessary for drawing up effective schedules.

Measuring results

As we have seen, few managers find planning a simple or immediately satisfying task. Although a structured framework for planning reduces the difficulty for managers and improves the quality of the planning, *adhering* to plans can still prove to be uphill work. But the temptations to veer off course must be resisted. Strategies and tactics relate to each other in a controlled and methodical fashion. Each step must be implemented in the light of previous steps and subsequent steps.

Careful monitoring will give clear comparisons between actual and planned performance. Variance can be assessed, its causes identified and necessary adjustments made in a methodical way, with a minimum of panic and a maximum of control.

Checklist

When deciding how to make the best use of its marketing resources, the organization should:

consider the benefits of a planned approach to its markets

decide what length of planning horizon would best meet its particular needs

ensure that marketing management does not neglect 'future' decisions

develop a systematic approach to marketing planning. This may involve carrying out a situation and SWOT analysis, making assumptions, setting marketing objectives, developing strategies and devising tactics, and then monitoring these plans.

26 Integrating and Co-ordinating Marketing Tools

Integrating what?

In the last chapter, mention was made of the importance of integrating the total marketing effort and co-ordinating marketing schedules. What does all this mean?

Part Three, you may remember, examined in some detail the ways in which the different marketing tools can be deployed by the organization to achieve success in the market-place.

Exercise: Take a moment now to jot down the names of the main marketing tools, along with a brief explanation of how and why each one is important.

If you've written down a brief summary of the four 'P's and mentioned as well the importance of marketing research, then you are quite justified in feeling pleased with yourself. If you hesitated over the question, or wrote something quite different, then you may want to look again at Parts Two and Three.

An understanding of each of these tools – and an appreciation of the various ways in which they can be used – is certainly extremely important to the successful marketer. Equally important, however, is the realization that the true value of each of the tools lies in its contribution to the marketing mix as a whole. Only if they are 'mixed' together in a balanced and supportive way can these four tools provide a kit for marketing success. The watchword for the marketer must be *integration of effort*.

Life without integration

What happens if the marketing tools *are* used independently or with little integration? The results can be summarized as follows:

1. The organization's marketing effort will *lack impact* in the market-place. For example, a fine product poorly distributed may never even reach the market; a good product which is wrongly priced (whether too high or too low) may have only a limited appeal for its intended target market; a brilliantly creative promotional message will have only a very short-term effect unless the product can fulfil the promises made.

2. The marketing effort will suffer from *poor continuity*. That is, disjointed marketing activity will lack any medium or long-term theme or direction. As a result, customers may become disastrously confused. For example, the promotional message may be changed so often that in the end it both fails to reach its intended target audience and offers no support to the product in maintaining customer loyalty.

3. Unintegrated marketing is extremely *wasteful of resources*. A company may decide on the spur of the moment to take part in a trade exhibition; afterwards, it may even be pleased with the result of its decision in terms of exposure and sales. However, the sad fact is that, had participation in the exhibition been properly planned and integrated with the rest of the marketing activity, the company would have had a great deal more to be pleased about. As it is, management has failed to use its resources to the best effect.

The underlying argument here is that while, on the face of it, unintegrated marketing can sometimes seem to be successful, integrated marketing will in fact always be more successful. If you remain unconvinced that success is relative, then think for a moment of similar situations in quite different areas of life. Having been quite satisfied with your old banger of a car, for example, you are given the opportunity to sit behind the wheel of one of the latest models of one of the best makes. How many of us, in that situation, would wish to stick with our old favourite?

The point of the illustration, of course, is to emphasize the fact that, although disjointed marketing may appear to perform satisfactorily, it will always be less effective, have less of an impact and generate fewer profits and sales than will fully integrated marketing.

Achieving integrated marketing

If we accept that fully integrated marketing is the only desirable kind of marketing to have, then how can it be achieved? The fundamental point is to remember that the tools of marketing are nothing more than component parts which have considerably less value and purpose when used in isolation, than when they are properly integrated. Through committing itself to a thorough planning process, marketing management can work out how these component parts may be brought together to make a complete whole. Indeed, the very purpose and nature of marketing planning focuses attention on achieving a well-integrated marketing effort.

Consideration of other situations can help to reveal the importance of this 'integrated whole'. Take our earlier example of a car engine: what is this but a collection of component parts – parts which become effective only when they are assembled together, each with its clear function in relation to the other components? And what about a group of sportsmen or women playing a team game? They really become effective only when they are moulded together as a team in which each person knows his or her function and role and how it fits into the team's overall pattern of play.

In the examples above, a change in any of the individual components clearly will change the composition of the whole. Different components in the car engine will result in a different performance by the car; different players in a sports team will result in different play and performance. Equally, different uses of the component tools of marketing will result in a different overall marketing activity.

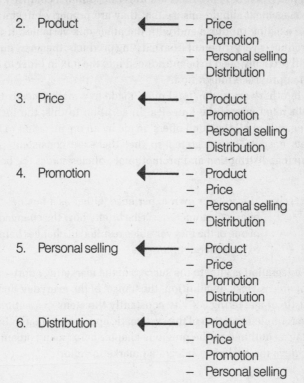

1. Market environment

2. Product ← – Price
                           – Promotion
                           – Personal selling
                           – Distribution

3. Price ← – Product
                           – Promotion
                           – Personal selling
                           – Distribution

4. Promotion ← – Product
                           – Price
                           – Personal selling
                           – Distribution

5. Personal selling ← – Product
                           – Price
                           – Promotion
                           – Distribution

6. Distribution ← – Product
                           – Price
                           – Promotion
                           – Personal selling

Figure 26.1. Integration of marketing elements

Marketing management should bear this fact constantly in mind. Any changes management makes to the components of the mix should be carried out with the total marketing picture in view. The marketing manager is in rather a similar position to that of a sporting coach who introduces a new player into the team. The manager/coach must ensure either that the new player adapts to the team method of play or that the team play changes to accommodate the new player.

Marketing integration, therefore, is about fitting the component parts together. As Figure 26.1 shows, products should be seen only in the context of price, promotion and place; while price should be seen only in the context of products, promotion and place . . . and so on. When new products are introduced into a company's range, management should ensure that they are properly integrated with the existing products and with the other mix variables. If the new product is very different from existing products, then new emphases will probably need to be introduced into the mix in order to achieve an appropriate integration.

In other words, the 'total offer' made to a market needs to be an integrated mix of the four 'P's. In addition to this, the individual elements of *all* the 'total offers' made by an organization to its markets need to be integrated so that there are consistent product, pricing, distribution and promotional policies across the board.

Exercise: From your own experience, either as a business person or as a customer, describe briefly how the changed nature of one of the mix variables resulted in changes being made to the other components.

Integration is vital to the success of the marketing effort – but it is not an easy task. In addition, the 'noise' of the everyday hustle and bustle of marketing activity constantly threatens distraction. However, implementation of the systematic approach to marketing planning as outlined in the previous chapter helps many organizations achieve the goal of an integrated marketing effort.

What needs to be co-ordinated?

Given that the whole marketing effort is integrated, what is there left to be co-ordinated? Basically, co-ordination is needed for the schedules of tactical activity which implement marketing strategies.

If you consider for a moment the many permutations possible in the marketing mix and the dynamic change constantly occurring in the market-place, then you will probably come to the conclusion that in fact marketing management has a considerable task of co-ordination on its hands. You will be quite right to make this judgement. Co-ordination is essential if all the situation-specific tactical marketing schedules are to add up to an efficient and effective marketing effort.

A number of areas have to be considered in assessing just how co-ordination can be introduced.

How should short-, medium and long-term plans and activities fit together? Lack of co-ordination in timing will lead to an eventual mismatching of marketing activities. Frequently companies which fail to pay full and proper attention to co-ordinating activities over time find that their annual marketing plan bears no relationship to what actually did happen over the period of the year.

How can planning be integrated with the marketing operation itself? In the absence of careful control and monitoring, planning activities can become detached from operational realities. And, as we have seen, unplanned operational activities quickly become haphazard, unintegrated and wasteful.

How can the promotional element be properly integrated into the mix? The urgent need to combat competition and exploit market forces means that promotional activity is all too often used on its own to make sudden forays into the market-place. In fact, moves of this kind are almost always counter-productive. Uncoordinated promotional activity all too easily leads to a mismatch and a shambles. For example, stocks available may be insufficient to meet customer demand, while various different promotional offers for the same product may serve only to confuse the customer.

In all these areas, the marketing function must co-ordinate its activities over time so that each activity is integrated with the whole and so that marketing events follow on from each other in a sensible way.

Co-ordinated marketing schedules follow a clear path towards a defined objective. You may find another analogy helpful here. Think of a rail or bus timetable. A train or bus will set off at a certain time towards a specific destination; it will complete the journey at a specified time. During the journey, it will stop at various points along the way – again, at specified times. A co-ordinated marketing schedule should follow a similar format and should be viewed in the same light. For example, we go to a railway station *expecting* the train to leave at a particular time; and we expect the journey to take a specific length of time. We should have similar expectations of our marketing schedule. Expecting to reach a particular point in a specified period of time, we will carry out specific and preplanned activities at certain points along the way. Such activities will help us to complete our journey successfully.

What might our schedule look like?

If we accept the importance of co-ordinated marketing schedules, then what *should* be the order of things, and what is the best way to achieve co-ordination? The answer must be that each organization's schedule will be different and unique to that firm's marketing activity. However, it can also be said that, for all organizations, the cornerstone of well-co-ordinated schedules will lie in effective and sound planning. The objectives and strategies established by the organization will in themselves dictate the order of events to some extent, although the precise order of particular events may vary to some degree depending on the strategy being followed. Good co-ordination backing up the marketing plan will ensure that each event is linked with others and results in a cumulative progression towards the objective.

Exercise: What is the main marketing objective of your own organization or of an organization well known to you? What sequence of marketing events must occur in order to achieve your objectives? Precisely when will these events occur? How will each event build upon previous events and support subsequent events?

In most organizations, the schedule itself will usually be drawn up on some sort of year-planner so that precise dates are given for each marketing action. In large companies which have many products and serve many markets, there may well be several schedules at different levels of detail. The important thing is that the schedule should tell each member of the marketing team exactly what should have happened by when, and what he or she should be doing and when.

Exercise: An example of a schedule is given in Figure 26.2 on p. 272. This was actually compiled and used by a firm. What improvements would you make to it? One might be to name who is responsible for what.

Checklist

To achieve the best result from their marketing activities, marketing managers must ensure that they:

appreciate the benefits of 'integrated' marketing

treat the marketing mix variables as inter-dependent parts of a whole

balance changes to one variable with appropriate changes to the other components

adopt a system of marketing planning which helps them to monitor the mix on a continual basis

decide how short-, medium and long-term plans fit together

ensure that planning is integrated with operational realities

ensure that the promotion element of the mix is not used in isolation from the other components

ensure that the co-ordination of operational schedules is treated as an essential element of the marketing planning process.

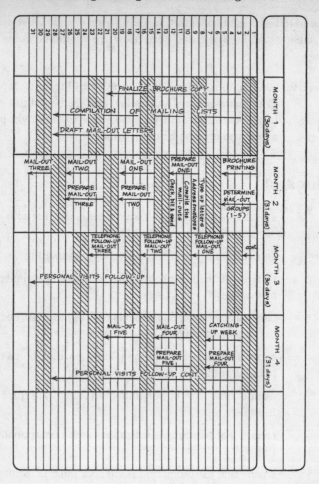

Figure 26.2.   Mail-out time schedule for A. N. Other product

27 Marketing Expenditure

Marketing expenditure: no one is immune

Every business that trades, and that supplies products to customers, spends money on marketing. There are no exceptions to this rule.

Think back for a moment to the opening chapters of this book. These emphasized the fact that *every* firm carries out marketing. The marketing may not be recognized as such; it may not be consciously undertaken; and it may not be good – but it does happen. When a businessman says that he does no marketing, the statement usually means that he does not use advertising or other obvious forms of promotion. However, that same businessman will usually agree that he is involved in all or most of the following activities:

> answering customer inquiries
>
> selling to customers
>
> setting prices
>
> delivering orders
>
> selecting and developing new products
>
> offering discounts.

The businessman is also most likely to have a letterheading, signwriting on vehicles and a company logo. In other words, he *is* involved in marketing – and this automatically means that he spends money and uses internal resources on marketing.

But just what *is* marketing expenditure? What does it include? The answer is far from clear-cut. In fact, most organizations do not know how much they spend on marketing.

Exercise: Suggest some reasons for this being the case.

Your thoughts should have been running along the following lines. In most organizations there are usually a good many activities which have an impact on customers and sales and which therefore have implications for marketing. This fact makes it difficult to distinguish which activities are properly counted as 'marketing' activities and should accordingly be included in marketing expenditure.

There are no textbook answers to questions such as whether packaging costs should be classified as a production or a marketing expense, or what proportion of distribution costs count as marketing costs. But there is a very important lesson to be learned from such deliberations. An organization's expenditure on marketing is always greater, and covers more areas, than the expenditure of the marketing department itself.

However, even businesses that acknowledge the wide scope of marketing activity rarely take this feature into account in the calculation of their marketing expenditure figures. More often they compromise by using one of the following yardsticks: (a) expenditure on 'obvious' marketing activities, or (b) expenditure by marketing and marketing-related functional departments.

Direct and indirect expenditure

There are basically two types of marketing expenditure.

(a)   Direct, out-of-pocket expenditure. This will typically include spending on such things as advertising space, promotional leaflets, and external market research reports.

(b)   Expenditure on internal resources – including people – used for marketing purposes. Examples here would include marketing's use of executive time, people, computer facilities and office space.

Most organizations are more sensitive to the former type of expenditure – which involves spending cash – than to the latter. However, the fact remains that the use of an organization's other scarce resources, such as time, effort, skill and facilities, involves equally high 'opportunity costs'.

Opportunity costs refer to the other possible uses of the resources which have to be forgone. The opportunity cost of a promotional campaign might be a new machine or an additional computer terminal. Needless to say, opportunity costs are encountered *within* marketing as well as across functional boundaries. For example, resources used on a new product launch cannot also be used to promote an existing line or to improve customer service.

An investment, not a cost

Although marketing expenditure does involve spending money, it is most appropriately viewed as an investment, rather than as a net cost. This is because the very aim and purpose of marketing is to yield more in profitable sales than it costs in resources.

Exercise: Despite this, the complaint is often levelled at marketing that it is a drain on resources – that is, a cost for the organization. Why might this complaint be made? Jot down a few ideas and then compare your explanation with the one that follows.

There are two main reasons for the attitude that marketing constitutes a cost. First, in some organizations marketing truly *is* little more than a cost. In such organizations, marketing is not undertaken in a planned, integrated and co-ordinated fashion, with each element building upon and supporting every other element. Instead, marketing is undertaken on a piecemeal basis without a cohesive framework. Resources are used spasmodically and on impulse, without any real attention being paid to how the different activities all fit together. The result, naturally enough, is little impact in the marketplace and even less return for the organization.

The second reason for this attitude concerns the time scale over which marketing returns are considered. Marketing should properly be viewed as a long-term activity, with returns accruing months and even years after the initial investment of resources. Indeed it is not uncommon for marketing undertaken in Year 1 to yield most of its returns in Years 2 and 3 – provided, of course, that the marketing in Years 2 and 3 supports rather than dissipates that of Year 1.

However, even with new product launches, the investment nature of marketing is in practice rarely acknowledged formally in a firm's financial reporting system. In fact, the contrary is the norm, with firms expecting marketing expenditure to be justified and covered by returns within the twelve-month period during which it is incurred. If the same criterion were applied to the purchase of machinery, it would mean working on a one-year pay-back period – an approach which no firm would dream of adopting.

Measuring return on investment

Obviously, every organization wants to achieve the best return on investment (ROI) possible from the resources it allocates to marketing. Despite the problems and limitations of many firms' data on marketing expenditure, insights into marketing performance can be gained through the use of comparative measures and ratios. For example, a comparison of the current year's sales and marketing expenditure with figures for previous years will *indicate* whether marketing funds are being used more or less effectively. The word 'indicate' is emphasized here because it is important for the firm to take account of any investment effect in its interpretation of the results of such comparison.

Expenditure and revenue by product group provide another set of materials for comparison. Inter-firm comparison too can be illuminating in this context. How much does Company A spend on advertising/market research/marketing training in comparison with Company B or the industry norm? How do these figures relate to sales and market-share figures for Companies A and B? These are the type of questions to be addressed when comparing a firm's marketing expenditure and returns with those of its competitors.

Comparison of marketing activities, expenditure and sales by customer type and market segment can also offer the firm a useful yardstick by which to judge the cost-effectiveness of its marketing. Through the use of this method the firm can, for example, assess the true opportunity cost of investing marketing resources in one segment rather than another. Market segment comparison also indicates the relative value-for-money of marketing expenditure in each segment in terms of sales revenue generated. However, to take advantage of this method, a firm needs accurate and detailed revenue and costing information broken down by market segments.

The marketing budget

In an attempt to control and systematize marketing expenditure, most organizations set an annual budget for marketing activities. When, as often happens, this budget is identical to the one allocated to the marketing department, this system encounters some of the obstacles described earlier in this chapter. In particular, the fact that marketing activities extend well beyond the frontiers of the marketing department itself presents a considerable stumbling block to the setting of a realistic budget.

So, how much should the organization spend on marketing? The answer must be: as much as is required and can be afforded. This figure can best be determined in the light of the insights offered by the comparison analysis. A sum related to sales revenue (such as x per cent of net revenue) is never a satisfactory solution. Such calculations do not relate marketing expenditure to market needs and can easily result in too much or too little being spent. (This argument will be familiar to you from the discussion on promotional budgeting in Chapter 24.)

Checklist

In attempting to assess and control its marketing expenditure, the organization should:

identify the full extent of its marketing activities

take into account both direct and indirect marketing expenditure, including the opportunity costs involved view marketing expenditure as an investment rather than a net cost

use methods such as comparison analysis to gain a clearer picture of the cost-effectiveness of its marketing activities.

28 Organizing for Marketing

Finding the right framework

By this stage of the book, you will have a clear idea of the importance to a firm of being customer-orientated and of following a planned approach to marketing, with clear objectives and strategies. You will also appreciate that marketing activities need to be integrated and co-ordinated in order to be truly effective – and that adequate resources, including time, must be set aside for their implementation.

However, there may be an underlying question still in your mind: 'Just how is all this supposed to come together within the organization?' or 'Is it necessary for an organization to have a marketing department to do marketing?' The simple answer to the second question is, 'Not necessarily.' Indeed, some managers take the view that marketing is far too important to a business to be left to a marketing department!

Thinking small to medium

The *size* of a business is one of the most important factors affecting the way marketing is organized. In small firms, and especially new businesses, the management often consists of only one or two people. For these people, 'marketing manager' is just one of the many hats worn in a working week. Such firms have neither the need nor the resources for specialist management.

As may readily be appreciated, in these circumstances the issue of organizing for marketing is one of time rather than of structure. Specifically, the question presents itself as to how willing management is to *make* time for marketing – particularly when it comes to planning for the future.

Solutions to this problem of finding, or making, time for marketing are many and various. Most are based on the principle of setting aside specific times for marketing thinking. One successful female entrepreneur dedicates the time she spends washing up after family dinners in the evening to her marketing thinking. The acquisition of a dishwasher has not been allowed to encroach on this! Whatever the solution, the impetus for finding it is always the same: the conviction that marketing (even if the word itself is never used) is a vital ingredient of commercial success. Where this conviction is lacking, time is not found and the firm tends to 'muddle through' with its marketing.

Exercise: Think of a small to medium-sized business that you know well. What are the attitudes of its personnel towards marketing? How does it organize its marketing and marketing planning? What improvements could be made to this system?

As businesses grow, more and more specialist managers are taken on board, with finance and production posts usually being the first to be filled. By the time a firm can be described as big, it will usually have found it necessary to formalize reporting structures and areas of managerial responsibility. And in the case of marketing, there will be not just the one specialist, but a whole department or section of specialists.

Thinking big

At this stage in most books on marketing, an organization chart such as Figure 28.1 is presented to illustrate a 'typical' structure for marketing in big business. Such 'typical' structures are rarely, if ever, found in practice; but they are, nevertheless, useful in providing an indication of the way in which responsibility for various aspects of marketing are allocated.

Exercise: Take a careful look at Figure 28.1. What sort of problems do you believe a firm with this type of organizational arrangement might encounter?

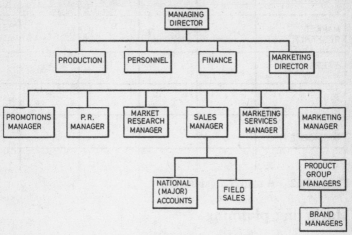

Figure 28.1.   A 'typical' organizational chart for marketing

One problem which you may have identified is the problem of co-ordination *within* the marketing function itself, as well as the integration and co-ordination of marketing within the organization as a whole. Co-ordination always becomes a problem when there is a combination of specialization and large groups of people; and both of these situations are implied by Figure 28.1.

Another observation about the diagram might be that it has as its starting point and focus the functional specialisms within marketing rather than market segments. There are product group and brand managers – but where are the market managers? It is interesting, if rather strange, that marketing, with its philosophy of customer/market orientation, should have devised for itself such a product-orientated organizational system as that of product or brand management.

OPERATIONAL	PLANNING TEAMS				
RESPONSIBILITIES	MARKET A	MARKET B	MARKET C	MARKET D	etc.
PROMOTION					
MARKET RESEARCH					
SALES					
P.R.					
BRAND MANAGEMENT					
etc.					

Figure 28.2.   A matrix organization

Marketing planning

How does marketing planning fit into this type of structure? Many organizations give each manager within the marketing
department (such as the advertising manager and sales manager) the
task of developing plans for his or her own area. The merit of this
approach is that each manager should have an intimate knowledge
of likely developments in his or her field. The drawback is that plans
can be developed independently of the whole marketing picture and
the overall composition of the marketing mix – unless, that is, there
is really effective umbrella co-ordination. Without careful balancing
and matching, a real danger of organized chaos exists.

State-of-the-art marketing planning has moved away from this
model to one which rests firmly on the building blocks of market
segment planning. The mechanism for developing such plans is the
'planning team' – each team having responsibility for developing
plans for particular market areas.

The composition of planning teams does vary. But where this
planning framework is superimposed on organizational frameworks
such as Figure 28.1, a matrix structure on the lines of Figure 28.2
tends to emerge. Planning teams are made up of people with day-to-
day operational responsibility in one field of marketing (such as

promotion or advertising) – but who within the planning framework focus attention on a market area rather than on a specific marketing activity.

Even with this approach to planning, overall co-ordination of market plans is required. But in this case, since the task is market-orientated, decisions on resource allocation and judgements on compatibility are automatically focused on markets rather than on functional areas of marketing.

There are, of course, disadvantages associated with this approach, too. Most of these stem from the inescapable fact that planning teams are essentially committees. You may remember the cynical old comment 'A camel is a horse designed by a committee'? It is often difficult to integrate the sometimes diverse knowledge and experience present in the same team, and to bring various viewpoints into harmony.

In short

What general conclusions can be drawn? First, if marketing and marketing planning are to be effective, then they must have their own niche within a company's organization structure, whatever the size and nature of the company. Secondly, the method employed for ensuring this will depend on the nature and size of the organization. Whichever planning mechanism is chosen must be compatible with the existing organization structure of the company.

Checklist

In assessing how its marketing can best be organized, the company should:

determine whether or not its size demands the existence of a formalized marketing structure

if it is a small firm, ensure that time is devoted to marketing and marketing planning if it is a larger firm, ensure that the structure chosen for the marketing function minimizes problems of co-ordination

explore the possible advantages of introducing a 'planning team' approach to marketing planning.

5 Marketing Issues

29 Marketing in Different Situations

What does 'different' mean?

How do you apply the fundamental concepts and pro-
cesses of marketing to particular situations? This is one of the most
difficult tasks facing the inexperienced marketer.

Usually, application of the concepts entails adaptation of the ideas
to suit the circumstances in question. However, such adaptation
should not be carried out before a careful analysis has been made of
these circumstances. The cardinal rule guiding this analysis is that
it should focus on market conditions and customer buying behaviour; it should *not* focus on the particular product being marketed.

What does this mean in practice? It means, simply, that no marketer should make the automatic assumption that his or her product
is somehow 'different' from all other products, especially in the field
of consumer products. An example from service marketing may help
to illustrate this point. Until fairly recently, the idea of selling life
insurance policies 'off the page' – that is, through coupons in newspapers, and so on – would have aroused scorn among many marketers of financial services. They would have argued that their
product – life insurance policies – required careful person-to-person
selling and could never be sold in the same way as, say, a set of
saucepans. In fact, the direct approach to selling life insurance
policies has proved hugely successful.

If the sceptical financial marketers referred to above had stopped to consider what their potential customers might actually *want* in the way of selling methods, they might have reached the right conclusion. As it was, they made the elementary mistake of looking at the product (and that through the eyes of tradition) and ignoring the customer.

Because of historical factors, marketing approaches and theories are often based on the practice and experience of large producers of fast-moving consumer goods (fmcgs, in the jargon). Let us follow tradition by using this as a starting point in looking at marketing in various contexts.

Consumer versus industrial marketing

The need to adapt the marketing mix may seem most apparent when we consider the differences between industrial and consumer marketing. The generally held wisdom is that it is folly to carry out marketing programmes of the same type in both these sectors because the buying characteristics of each are so different. But are they really?

Exercise: Take a moment to jot down what you understand to be the main characteristics of buyers in (a) consumer markets, and (b) industrial markets.

Thinking back to Chapter 7 on buying, you will remember that industrial buyers are often typified as being more economically rational than consumers. But you will also remember it being noted that industrial buyers, like consumers, are subject to habit buying; and that they are not immune to a whole range of influences (such as internal politics) on their buying decisions. Nevertheless, industrial buyers do aspire to making economically sound and logical buying decisions; and, even if the actual decisions do not live up to this aspiration, those involved in industrial marketing need to appreciate and work with this self-image and tailor their messages accordingly.

Industrial markets differ from consumer markets in other important respects, including:

the existence of fewer potential customers

the large number of people involved in buying decisions

the likelihood that the buyer will be knowledgeable and well informed

the greater average value of orders placed.

The combination of all these factors means that in the field of promotion, for instance, advertising copy needs to be less emotive in tone; and there will tend to be a greater emphasis put on personal selling, trade press advertising, trade fairs and exhibitions, and the technical brochure.

However, while taking care to bear in mind differences between the two types of market, marketers should not fall into the trap of over-emphasizing the differences. Nor should they underplay the diversity within different *industrial* markets. For example, the marketing of computers to industry is very different from the marketing of paper-clips to industry. Indeed, the marketing of computers to industry probably has more in common with the marketing of expensive, technical consumer goods such as hi-fis, cameras and personal computers.

Marketing services

Another field in which traditional marketing ideas are said to need considerable adaptation is where the product is a service rather than 'goods'.

Unlike goods, services are physically intangible; in other words, they cannot be touched, tasted, seen or smelt. But why should this matter? After all, you will recall from earlier chapters that customers are primarily concerned with the *benefits* a product yields. And services yield benefits just as goods do.

Despite this, the lack of tangibility *is* an important factor in marketing services. Customers seem to find it more difficult to grasp just what is being offered – and to distinguish between one service offer and another. With furniture, for instance, it is possible to see what the product is and to compare, say, several tables at various prices. But, with decorators, it is less easy to establish just what the charge for redecorating a room includes – and to compare the differences in service offered by various decorators quoting different prices.

This difficulty in defining exactly what constitutes a service can quickly lead to customer anxiety about the service itself and, subsequently, to a negative attitude towards it. Just think of the number of services about which customers tend to be sceptical. Solicitors, estate agents and garages are just three service providers often accused of giving less than value for money.

Because of this phenomenon, those involved in marketing services are always looking for ways of making a service seem more concrete, more 'real'. For instance, the hotel that puts drinking glasses in clean paper bags, provides a new wrapped tablet of soap and attaches 'cleaned' bands across bath, basin and toilet is providing tangible evidence of the room being specially cleaned and prepared for the new occupant.

Other characteristics of services that have a special bearing on the marketing approaches used include the following:

> services cannot be standardized to the same extent as physical goods

> services cannot be produced before they are required and then stored to meet demand.

Non-profit organizations and marketing

Marketing in non-profit sectors provides another distinct marketing context. The objective of traditional marketing, in line with that of commercial activity generally, is the pursuit of profit. The objective of non-profit marketing, by contrast, is usually the promotion of an attitude or a cause. Marketing other than for profit is practised in such fields as health, education, public amenities and government. Politics and religion are also areas where there is growing evidence of marketing activity – although it is rarely acknowledged as such.

Intangibility is perhaps an even more salient factor in the non-profit field than in the marketing of services. Frequently the desired outcome is the creation of an attitude, rather than a purchase. The publishers of health books and the proprietors of health clubs may benefit indirectly from the Health Council's marketing activity. However, the end 'product' being promoted by the Health Council is 'healthy living'.

Some forms of non-profit marketing offer no direct benefits to the consumer. Campaigns by charities, for instance, often appeal to the altruism of the donor, whose reward may be 'in heaven' or in his or her good conscience. Certainly, it does not come directly from the charity. Success in these areas, where benefits are at best intangible, indirect and even abstract, provides perhaps the greatest challenge to the non-profit marketer.

In other spheres of non-profit marketing, there is no purchase involvement by the consumer – with obvious implications for the management of the four 'P's. Take the example of social services. What is the price of a service? Who are the customers? And what is the product? How do you judge the success of any marketing? It is clear that the marketing context here demands quite a radical adaptation of the marketing concepts.

Another difference with some non-profit marketing is the nature of the competition. With the National Health Service or education, the competition is provided by other organizations providing the same or similar products – private health, private schools, other colleges and universities. This follows the same pattern as the commercial sector. But often with non-profit marketing, the competitors are organizations promoting different attitudes or products. With the government's anti-smoking campaign, for instance, the competition comprises tobacco companies rather than other anti-smoking groups like ASH. In order to succeed, the campaign's promotion and message must oust the competition offered by the tobacco companies. The image of smoking as glamorous, fashionable and so on must be replaced by another image: that of smoking as seedy, immature, foolish, old-fashioned and unhealthy.

Small business marketing

Small businesses are not simply little big businesses. Smallness gives businesses their own particular characteristics and hence their own marketing strengths and weaknesses. This means that while all the concepts of marketing apply to small, medium and large firms equally, their interpretation into practical marketing tends to be very different.

By definition, small firms have limited resources. They also usually have limited marketing awareness and knowledge. This means that marketing activities have to be inexpensive and simple. Small firms just cannot afford such things as extensive field research or intensive television advertising; because of this, they often feel themselves to be at a disadvantage.

The small firm does, however, have many marketing advantages; and the secret of small business market success is to build on these advantages rather than try to ape the inappropriate big business marketing practices.

One of the main strengths of small firms is their *flexibility*. They can respond quickly to changes in customer requirements and market needs. Furthermore, because decision-makers have closer contact with customers than do decision-makers in large firms, the need for change can be recognized and acted upon more quickly.

The flexibility of small firms, along with their lack of inhibiting rules and procedures, offers further advantages. Such firms find it easier to experiment in the market-place and to handle non-standard orders; this means that more customized products can be offered – often a very profitable line of business.

Sometimes, however, small firms dissipate these advantages by initiating too many different activities and by trying to serve the needs of too many different types of customers. Small firms do not have the resources to spread a wide net; they need to concentrate their marketing efforts.

Retailing

Manufacturers are more concerned with *what* people buy than *where* they buy. As long as the customer buys his product, a manufacturer is not interested in the identity of the intermediary from whom the purchase is made. The opposite is true of retailers. Retailers are more concerned with *where* people buy than *what* they buy. As long as the items are bought from one of his outlets, the retailer is relatively indifferent as to which particular items are purchased.

This difference in orientation explains why marketing by retailers differs from manufacturer marketing. Take the 'product' element of the mix, for instance. To the retailer, the product is the outlet – it is the outlet which has to be sold to consumers. Management of the product 'P' therefore means getting 'right' the store location and premises, the assortment of products for sale, store layout and design, the image of value for money, and the customer service provided by shop staff.

The 'promotion' element of the mix is in turn geared towards building store loyalty as opposed to brand loyalty – although retailers happily use branded goods prices to help them achieve this goal. It is interesting to note how in recent years retailer advertising has become more sophisticated and extensive, in line with retailer marketing in general. Think, for example, of multiple stores like Sainsbury's and Asda. Although full-page advertisements in local papers setting out special-offer prices are still used, this is no longer the sole form of advertising. Today, local advertising is used alongside image-building advertising on television and in magazines which focuses on aspects like the freshness and range of fruit and vegetables, the quality of the provisions and the standard of the service.

Retailers also price products differently from manufacturers. In general, retailers use standard mark-ups; they stock simply too many lines to allow individual product pricing. However, retailers do vary mark-ups and prices. Higher-priced and slower-moving lines generally have higher mark-ups than fast-moving cheap lines. In addition, retailers cut prices and margins of popular lines for promotional purposes – the 'loss leader' being a case in point.

International marketing

With marketing to customers overseas, differences in approach become both apparent and real. Most marketers realize at an early stage that in entering markets with different traditions, customs, languages, and so on, they must make an effort to appreciate the full significance of the changed environment. Although such differences present a considerable challenge, they also serve to provide marketers with a clear early warning that they are now playing in a different ball-game and will have to discard many of their usual assumptions.

The principles of marketing still hold good for overseas activity, but special attention must be paid to:

> acquiring understanding and knowledge of customers and markets

> getting the *details* of marketing activities right

> understanding the various legal and trade requirements involved.

The distance involved in international marketing means that the organization often has less direct control of the marketing mix. The use of agents or intermediaries is frequently essential; hence the appointment of efficient agents is often the single most important step in building up an effective marketing operation.

Checklist

In assessing whether – or how – marketing principles should be adapted to meet particular situations, marketers should:

> analyse the relevant market conditions and patterns of customer buying behaviour

> familiarize themselves with the *real* differences in:
> consumer marketing
> industrial marketing
> service marketing

marketing by non-profit organizations
small business marketing
marketing by retailers
international marketing.

30 Ethics and Marketing

What ethics?

Throughout this book we have put forward a professional and logical approach to marketing. By providing a framework for sound marketing practice, we have attempted to indicate how marketing personnel can harness their intuitive skills to good effect. We have described and urged 'correct' approaches to all aspects of marketing.

The first hint of a flaw in the marketing edifice was raised in the last chapter, when we dared to suggest that the theory can be somewhat different from the reality and practice of marketing. It must further be recognized that pressures of survival – sales, profits, competition, job security, and so on – leave marketing, perhaps more than any other business function, susceptible to a lowering of standards and unethical behaviour.

Of course it is all very fine to talk about ethics in business and marketing, but is there such a thing? Is it realistic to *expect* ethical behaviour, given all the pressures in the market place?

Exercise: Take a moment now to jot down your own thoughts on this matter.

Ethics in business and commerce are expressed, in broad terms, through 'rules of conduct'. Other professions certainly have rules of this kind: doctors, accountants, and lawyers all spring to mind. But does marketing have similar controls? It might be argued that there are established rules and codes of practice – for example, the Advertising Standards Association's Legal, Decent, Honest and Truthful Code, and the newspapers' Mail Order Protection Scheme – M.O.P.S. These codes do indeed play an important part in maintaining standards and creating and maintaining consumer confidence. But do they get to the heart of the matter?

Let us consider for a moment the kind of 'image' marketing has in society and among the business fraternity in general. What about advertising, for example? In his book *Advertising Management*, Doyle lists eight criticisms of advertising:

1. Advertising exhibits bad taste
2. Advertising is frequently false and misleading
3. Advertising stresses small and insignificant differences between products and has resulted in an unnecessary and wasteful proliferation of brands
4. Advertising has resulted in uniformity
5. Advertising concentrates on selling people products they neither need nor want
6. Advertising is too persuasive
7. Much advertising is irrelevant and unnecessary
8. Advertising can be used to take advantage of children.

This looks like a damning indictment of one major aspect of marketing; and in fact it is not difficult to find examples which bear out the critics.

In relation to some of the above charges, you will probably all agree that it is right to demand high standards. No one wants to be misled by an advertisement. A case in point is that of an advertisement for a slimming loaf in which it was claimed that each slice had fewer calories than other slimming loaves. What the advertisement failed to point out was that this was merely because the slices were smaller and thinner. In this case the advertisement fell foul of advertising standards in the USA.

On the other hand, would we necessarily agree that it is wrong for advertising to stress 'small and insignificant differences between products', as stated in point 3 above? It could be argued that advertising opens up to the customer a tremendous variety of choice in the market-place by doing this.

Such questions perhaps represent the tip of the iceberg, the unseen bulk of which, below the waterline, involves issues much bigger than marketing alone. These issues include questions of how the economy and society as a whole should be organized, free market capitalism versus state intervention, and so forth.

These larger issues are beyond the scope of this book. The fact is that we live in a society in which goods and services are produced for the open market, so that marketing, whether good or bad, well or badly organized, ethical or disgraceful, will inevitably take place.

Personal ethics

Marketing itself can perhaps best be seen as an ethically neutral activity. Its methods can plainly be used for good or for ill. Promotional techniques, for instance, can be geared to selling both confectionery which rots our teeth and bran-packed breakfast cereals which (if the nutritionists have got it right) do us a power of good.

So where does this leave us as individuals who have an interest in marketing? Ethical standards are ultimately a matter of personal conscience as well as of corporate policy. We may or may not believe that the standards put forward by, for instance, the Advertising Standards Association are high enough.

Exercise: Ask yourself whether you would be happy to work in marketing for a confectionery company. Do you see anything desperately wicked in it? Your answer may well depend on your own eating habits! But what about cigarettes? Where would you, personally, draw the line? Think about your own ethical standards and how these compare with what the profession and our society as a whole seem prepared to accept. Draw on your own experience of television and other advertising and of the different sorts of controversial products that you know are on sale, ranging from fur coats and 'adult' magazines to high-tech weapons systems.

The important thing in this analysis is not whether any of these products is intrinsically 'ethical' or 'unethical'. That could be the cue for endless debate. What is important to anyone going into marketing is to be clear in their own mind about the issues of conscience that they might have to face in any particular marketing role, and how they would react 'when it comes to the crunch'. Some 'crunch' situations, of course, can be avoided by a refusal to take work in areas which cause uneasiness.

Some products would rarely be considered harmful in themselves but nevertheless may be the focus for considerable moral qualms. The conditions endured by workers on certain tea plantations, for example, are revealed from time to time to be seriously substandard. And fashion garments are not infrequently made up by very poorly paid outworkers.

How do you as a consumer feel about such products? Do you believe that there would be a substantial change in these feelings if you were actually involved in marketing the products?

There can be yet another ethical 'angle' to a situation in which the products themselves are not considered harmful. In some cases, the actual *methods* used to promote and sell the products may be regarded as morally dubious. Some people would argue, for instance, that the 'hard sell' techniques associated with some double glazing or encyclopedia firms exploit the fears and insecurities of vulnerable sections of the community.

The poor image marketing has

Whatever your personal feelings, you will probably have encountered an underlying negative attitude to marketing among many people. Marketing does not enjoy such public esteem as, say, the medical profession. The image tends to be one of dubious practice. Ask any consumer, 'Would you trust a second-hand car dealer?', or, similarly, 'Would you believe everything an estate agent tells you?' It may well be that the great majority of car dealers and estate agents are honest, trustworthy and reliable, but the fact remains that they do not have a good 'image' in society.

This poor image permeates marketing. It is a sad truth that several adverse characteristics can easily be identified and related to by society and business alike. There is, for instance, the 'catch at all costs' approach to marketing, where the executive's sole purpose is to secure the sale, regardless of post-purchase evaluation – an approach hardly in keeping with the marketing philosophy developed in these pages. and then there is the 'wolf in sheep's clothing' syndrome, where the executive parades as an honest broker, suggesting that his sole purpose is to help and serve the customer even if he gains nothing for himself.

A myriad similar negative images of marketing probably float in the public imagination. But is marketing doing anything substantive to dispel them? Is it, or will it be, possible to have such things as rules of conduct in marketing? Can the marketing executive be ethical and remain effective?

It is probable that marketing will never dispose of the cowboy operators and exploiters of consumer weaknesses. Where there is an opportunity to 'make a fast buck' there will be people striving to do so, regardless of codes of practice, rules or ethics. But the future is likely to see a trend towards better marketing behaviour and practice. A multiplicity of factors, including enlightened self-interest, will contribute to this development.

As their influence becomes steadily more widespread throughout the business world, the growing disciplines of marketing and public relations are encouraging companies to reflect more deeply on how their long-term survival depends on their nurturing a good reputation. Nor is this a matter of striving for a good company 'image' without any substance behind it. Good marketing and PR texts always emphasize that poor products, poor after-sales service, and so on, are substantive matters that lead to customer dissatisfaction and disillusionment, and ultimately to customers voting with their feet by buying elsewhere.

Another of the major influences on change lies in the attitudes of the consumers themselves. Consumerism has had a tremendous impact on marketing behaviour. Consumer legislation will continue to combat unscrupulous marketers, but it is the general trend towards better standards that will perhaps have the greatest influence on improved ethics in marketing.

Consumers are increasingly asking for, and expecting to get, better products and services. Indeed in many areas (although certainly not all), products today are of better quality than ever before, and it is this enhanced quality and the demand for it that may eventually see the demise of unscrupulous marketing. Take only one area as an example: the motor car. Car manufacturers today are offering up to three years' warranty on mechanical performance and six years' warranty on body corrosion. Warranties on second-hand cars are now commonplace. Ten or fifteen years ago, such reliability would have been unheard of. In another ten or fifteen years, it is possible that warranties may extend even further.

In tandem with this improved quality, manufacturers are extending their control of after-sales service and second-hand sales service in line with the longer life cars now have. Consequently, we are seeing the growth of approved dealership for second-hand cars. The effect of this is to improve the marketing and customer service of the second-hand car dealer and also to squeeze out the dubious operators. Certainly, there are fewer back-street dealers in existence today than there were ten years ago.

Marketing professionalism

Similar kinds of improvements in marketing performance are occurring in many other industries; and there is no doubt that these will continue, in line with increased consumer sophistication and discerning purchasing patterns. If marketing is to meet the new demands and expectations of society, the message is clear: it must put its house in order; it must become more professional; it must strive to be better respected as a profession.

This new professionalism may require an ethical development on the part of marketers; that is, those in the marketing profession may have to make a conscious effort to strive for better market offerings and more honest messages. One objective should be to offer the consumer something that is better than expected, rather than to state that an offering is better than it really is.

Checklist

In considering the ethical implications of marketing activity, you will probably want to:

study the criticisms levelled against advertising and assess their validity in the light of your own experience identify other areas of marketing which strike you as susceptible to ethical controversy

decide how you stand on those issues

explore opportunities in which you can promote high standards as commercially beneficial

analyse how well your organization responds to complaints from customers.

FOR THE BEST IN PAPERBACKS, LOOK FOR THE

In every corner of the world, on every subject under the sun, Penguin represents quality and variety – the very best in publishing today.

For complete information about books available from Penguin – including Pelicans, Puffins, Peregrines and Penguin Classics – and how to order them, write to us at the appropriate address below. Please note that for copyright reasons the selection of books varies from country to country.

In the United Kingdom: For a complete list of books available from Penguin in the U.K., please write to *Dept E.P., Penguin Books Ltd, Harmondsworth, Middlesex, UB7 0DA*

In the United States: For a complete list of books available from Penguin in the U.S., please write to *Dept BA, Penguin, 299 Murray Hill Parkway, East Rutherford, New Jersey 07073*

In Canada: For a complete list of books available from Penguin in Canada, please write to *Penguin Books Canada Ltd, 2801 John Street, Markham, Ontario L3R 1B4*

In Australia: For a complete list of books available from Penguin in Australia, please write to the *Marketing Department, Penguin Books Australia Ltd, P.O. Box 257, Ringwood, Victoria 3134*

In New Zealand: For a complete list of books available from Penguin in New Zealand, please write to the *Marketing Department, Penguin Books (NZ) Ltd, Private Bag, Takapuna, Auckland 9*

In India: For a complete list of books available from Penguin, please write to *Penguin Overseas Ltd, 706 Eros Apartments, 56 Nehru Place, New Delhi, 110019*

In Holland: For a complete list of books available from Penguin in Holland, please write to *Penguin Books Nederland B.V., Postbus 195, NL–1380AD Weesp, Netherlands*

In Germany: For a complete list of books available from Penguin, please write to *Penguin Books Ltd, Friedrichstrasse 10 – 12, D–6000 Frankfurt Main 1, Federal Republic of Germany*

In Spain: For a complete list of books available from Penguin in Spain, please write to *Longman Penguin España, Calle San Nicolas 15, E–28013 Madrid, Spain*

FOR THE BEST IN PAPERBACKS, LOOK FOR THE

PENGUIN REFERENCE BOOKS

The Penguin Guide to the Law

This acclaimed reference book is designed for everyday use, and forms the most comprehensive handbook ever published on the law as it affects the individual.

The Penguin Medical Encyclopedia

Covers the body and mind in sickness and in health, including drugs, surgery, history, institutions, medical vocabulary and many other aspects. 'Highly commendable' – *Journal of the Institute of Health Education*

The Penguin French Dictionary

This invaluable French-English, English-French dictionary includes both the literary and dated vocabulary needed by students, and the up-to-date slang and specialized vocabulary (scientific, legal, sporting, etc) needed in everyday life. As a passport to the French language, it is second to none.

A Dictionary of Literary Terms

Defines over 2,000 literary terms (including lesser known, foreign language and technical terms) explained with illustrations from literature past and present.

The Penguin Map of Europe

Covers all land eastwards to the Urals, southwards to North Africa and up to Syria, Iraq and Iran. Scale – 1:5,500,000, 4-colour artwork. Features main roads, railways, oil and gas pipelines, plus extra information including national flags, currencies and populations.

The Penguin Dictionary of Troublesome Words

A witty, straightforward guide to the pitfalls and hotly disputed issues in standard written English, illustrated with examples and including a glossary of grammatical terms and an appendix on punctuation.

FOR THE BEST IN PAPERBACKS, LOOK FOR THE 🐧

PENGUIN BUSINESS

Great management classics of the world (with brand new Introductions by leading contemporary figures); widely studied business textbooks; and exciting new business titles covering all the major areas of interest for today's businessman and businesswoman.

Parkinson's Law or **The Pursuit of Progress** C. Northcote Parkinson
My Years with General Motors Alfred P. Sloan Jr
Self-Help Samuel Smiles
The Spirit of Enterprise George Gilder
Dinosaur & Co: Studies in Corporate Evolution Tom Lloyd
Understanding Organizations Charles B. Handy
The Art of Japanese Management Richard Tanner Pascale & Anthony G. Athos
Modern Management Methods Ernest Dale & L. C. Michelon
Lateral Thinking for Management Edward de Bono
The Winning Streak Workout Book Walter Goldsmith & David Clutterbuck
The Social Psychology of Industry J. A. C. Brown
Offensive Marketing J. H. Davidson
The Anatomy of Decisions Peter G. Moore & H. Thomas
The Human Side of Enterprise Douglas McGregor
Corporate Recovery Stuart Slatter